The Frugal
Woodturner

The Frugal Woodturner

MAKE AND MODIFY ALL THE TOOLS AND EQUIPMENT YOU NEED

Ernie Conover

Fox Chapel
PUBLISHING

ISBN 978-1-56523-434-5

Library of Congress Cataloging-in-Publication Data

Conover, Ernie.

The frugal woodturner / by Ernie Conover
      p. cm.

Includes index.

ISBN: 978-1-56523-434-5

1. Turning (Lathe work) 2. Lathes. 3. Woodwork I. Title.

TT201.C657 2010
684'.--dc22

                        2009049372

To learn more about the other great books from Fox Chapel Publishing, or to find a retailer near you, call toll-free 800-457-9112 or visit us at *www.FoxChapelPublishing.com*.

Note to Authors: We are always looking for talented authors to write new books in our area of woodworking, design, and related crafts. Please send a brief letter describing your idea to Acquisition Editor, 1970 Broad Street, East Petersburg, PA 17520.

Printed in Indonesia
First printing: April 2010
Second printing: April 2011

Dedication

This book is dedicated to my very good friend and colleague King Heiple· I first met King in 1991 when he took my weeklong general turning class at Conover Workshops·

An about-to-retire orthopedic surgeon, King was exploring turning as a retirement hobby· Well before class started, he appropriated the lathe closest to mine and watched me like a hawk throughout the week· In fact, he would look so closely as I turned, I feared for his safety at times· All of this was simply a manifestation of King's keen powers of observation· He would go to his lathe and duplicate my work in a most workman-like manner·

During that week, we developed an affinity for each other, and in coming months found we shared much in common· We both possessed a good set of hand skills, as well as a love of firearms and shooting· Above all, we were both keenly interested in all things scientific and philosophical·

After that turning class, King's turning skills blossomed· Good hand skills combined with a discerning eye for artistic design had him taking first place in shows frequently· When I asked him if he would give me a hand with turning classes, he quickly agreed· Our students have been the benefactors ever since· Like Jack Sprat and his wife, I like spindle turning, while King is all about bowls· Coming from a craft background, I let the student struggle for a while before stepping in· King, coming from a medical background, is all over a mistake *before* it happens. The result is that together, we have the students scraping the platters clean.

—Ernie Conover, January 2010

Contents

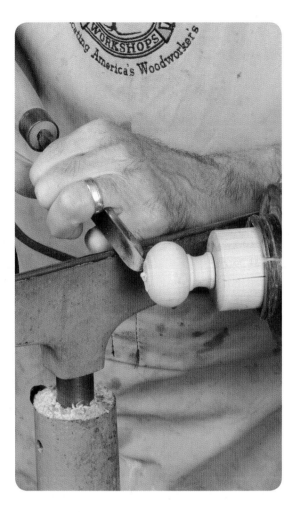

What You Can Learn From This Book:

How to Select the Right Size Lathe, Page 15

How to Make Your Own Spring Pole Lathe, Page 18

How to Make Your Own Lathe Stand, Page 37

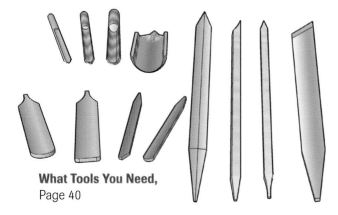

What Tools You Need, Page 40

How to Find Good Tools Without Breaking the Bank, Page 38

How to Make Your Own Tool Handles and Save Money, Page 58

How to Sharpen Spindle Gouges, Page 72

How to Sharpen a Bowl Gouge, Page 73

How to Find Free or Cheap Wood, Page 82

How to Keep Wood on the Lathe, Page 88

How to Make Your Own Faceplate, Page 92

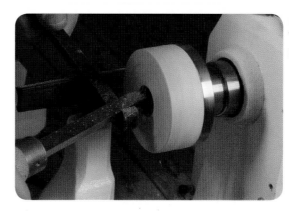

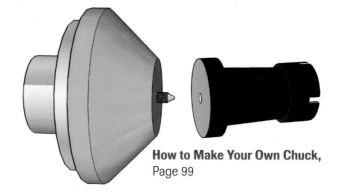

How to Make Your Own Chuck, Page 99

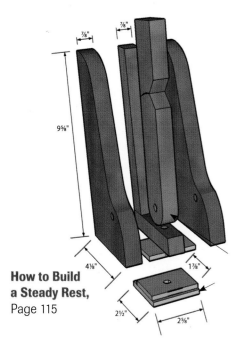

How to Build a Steady Rest, Page 115

7⁄8"
7⁄8"
9⁵⁄8"
4¹⁄8"
1⁷⁄8"
2½"
2⁵⁄8"

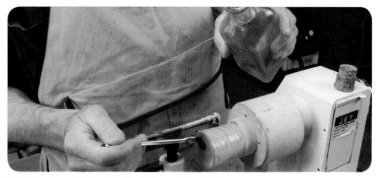

The Basics of Simple Finishes, Page 120

Introduction

These days, anyone who decides to try woodturning as a hobby might quickly decide it is just too expensive. That is a great shame, for turning actually is within the reach of everybody. What is more, improvising your own turning equipment from easily found or low-cost items can give you as much pleasure as the act of turning itself.

If you do that, you will be carrying on a fine tradition. In the past, woodturners routinely made many of their tools and all their chucks. Basement turners of my boyhood got by with little more than a bench lathe, a grinder for tool sharpening, and a band saw to cut rounds and blanks.

Turning Today: Pay to Play

Turning today is in danger of becoming gentrified. Machines are turnkey; you can practically plunk them down, plug them in, and start them up. Where turners of the past collected old chisels and files to grind into scrapers, many people today buy them. However, if you do not have the knowledge and skills to make a scraper from scratch, you lack the ability to sharpen the one you purchase.

I think you get much more satisfaction from making your own tools, benches, and chucks than from writing a check or handing over a credit/debit card to get the same gear ready-made. Making much of what you need for woodturning brings far better understanding of the process of turning itself. This book will break you free from the fetters of commercialism. It is also my fervent hope it will preserve a lot of information that may otherwise be lost.

The Appeal of Woodturning

Turning has long been a popular hobby because it does not require a lot of money, does not take up a lot of space, and consumes only a small amount of wood—often what is being thrown away by other users.

Turning is also an appealing hobby because it lets you make a useful article in a few hours or a weekend. Pens, rolling pins, bowls, and jars make great gifts or can become a source of income from your hobby.

I think turners divide into two camps—those who want to use turning to further their general woodworking and those who view turning as an end in itself. I will speak to both camps in this book.

Almost any woodworker can benefit from an ability to turn wood. Turning brings refinement as well as art to furniture in the form of columns, legs, stretchers, pulls, corner blocks, finials, pendants, bobs, and tabletops. Woe is the Windsor or Shaker chairmaker who cannot turn.

Those who pursue turning as an end in itself are what I call pure turners. They create objects made almost entirely with the lathe. These can be practical articles such as pens, candlesticks, rolling pins, clothespins, pasta cutters, honey dippers, spoons, forks, spatulas, platters, and bowls. They can be playthings like kaleidoscopes and tops. And they can be sculptural pieces whose size and shape is limited only by your imagination and the size of your lathe.

How This Book Will Help You

In order to be a woodturner, you need a lathe, of course. You can pay anywhere from a couple of hundred dollars to about $9,000 for a lathe, but my advice focuses on affordable equipment—new, used, or even homemade. I'll explain what you need to know to make good buying decisions for new or used equipment.

If you're starting from scratch, you'll need between 100 and 250 square feet (9 to 23 square meters) of floor space in the shop. This allows for a lathe, grinder, workbench, and a band saw. The workbench can be any sturdy table, but in the long run you will want a stout bench with a serviceable woodworking vise. If you are already a woodworker, you probably have a bench and a band saw, so you only need enough space for the lathe.

You will need between $150 and $500 worth of turning tools. It is best to begin with a few tools and add more as your budget and ability dictate. I will give you a complete rundown on tools, including ones you can make yourself. I will also give you the basic information you need to sharpen your tools, using a bench grinder and a versatile jig.

You *don't* need an expensive array of commercial chucks and faceplates to hold the work on the lathe. I will show you how to make your own for pennies. Not only will that improve your woodturning skills overall, it will give you chucks that are tailored to the exact type of woodturning you do.

I will also discuss how to find free or inexpensive wood for spindles and bowls, and how to turn green wood without having your work split and crack as the wood dries. I will show you how to apply three simple, inexpensive finishes.

Finally, I offer recommendations for outfitting a turning shop on three budgets, beginning with as little as $500 for a lathe and tools.

Throughout the book, I point out ways you can save money and still accomplish it all. By being a savvy buyer you will be a thrifty buyer. I will also suggest how you can buy now with upgrades in mind so that your equipment does not hinder your growth and development as a woodturner.

One more thing books, videos, and classes often overlook is practice. The most important thing that will make you a turner is to do a lot of turning. It is just like learning to play the piano. You can buy an expensive instrument and hire the best teachers, but you have to want to play. Above all, you have to practice.

1 Choosing the Right Lathe

The lathe constitutes the single most expensive item in a woodturning setup, so it is essential to know what qualities separate mediocre lathes from top-notch models. I will show you a gallery of very suitable, reasonably priced machines for a beginner. I also will outline what features and specifications offer the best value, to help you sort through manufacturers' claims. You will gain the knowledge to make wise purchasing choices, especially if you are shopping for used equipment.

The fact is, the lathe is a simple tool—many people make their own. You can, too. In this chapter, you'll find complete plans for a foot-powered pole lathe you can build in a weekend. There are also plans you can use to make your own lathe stand—a better, less-expensive alternative to commercial stands.

In this photo from the 2007 Powermatic Annual Report, author Ernie Conover stands with the Powermatic 3520b lathe, which he helped design. The photo in the background is of Ernie's father next to a Conover Lathe, which they designed together. Photo by Don Snyder

The Setup for a Typical Lathe

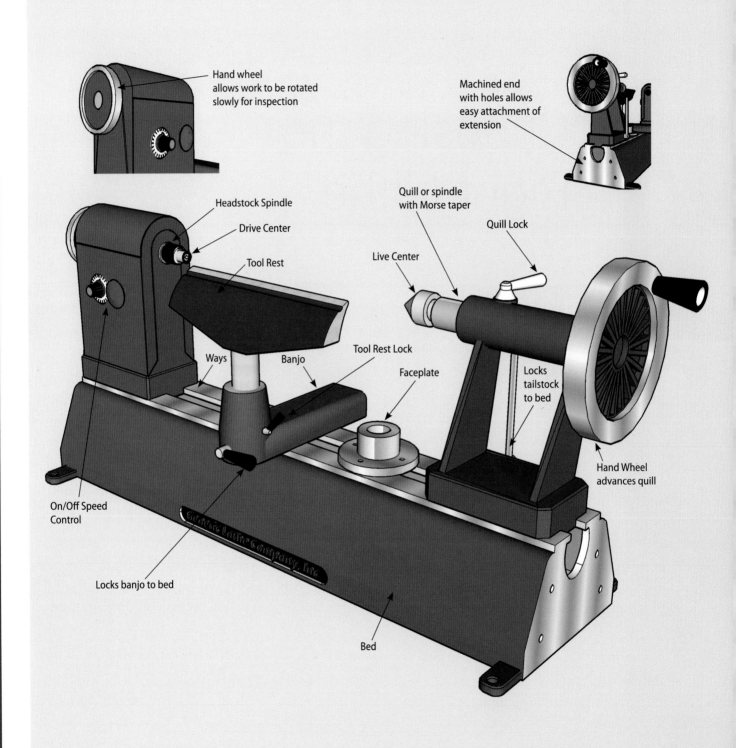

Hand wheel allows work to be rotated slowly for inspection

Machined end with holes allows easy attachment of extension

Headstock Spindle

Drive Center

Tool Rest

Quill or spindle with Morse taper

Quill Lock

Live Center

Ways

Banjo

Tool Rest Lock

Faceplate

Locks tailstock to bed

Hand Wheel advances quill

On/Off Speed Control

Locks banjo to bed

Bed

Generic Lathe Company, Inc

Lathe Types, Small to Large

The crucial parts of a lathe are the bed, the headstock, the tailstock, the banjo (tool base), and the tool rest. You also need a stand or bench to support the lathe. In the past, manufacturers divided lathes into two groups. *Heavy-duty* models were supplied with a stand. *Bench-top* models, used by amateurs and small shops, came without a stand.

Today, though, almost all lathes offer an optional stand. You will find two basic sizes—mini- and full-size. Bench-top lathes have nearly disappeared, with only a couple of models still on the market.

With either size, two important specifications are swing and bed length, which tell you how large a piece you can turn. Swing refers to the largest diameter of work the lathe can accommodate, while bed length dictates the maximum distance between the centers of the headstock and tailstock.

The mini-lathe. Small and relatively inexpensive, mini-lathes are well suited for turning spindles and small bowls. This one has a bed extension attached, giving it the capacity to turn long spindles.

MINI-LATHES—ABOUT $250 TO $500

Many people believe the popular mini-lathe was designed for miniature turning only; however, most mini-lathes can also handle full-size work.

Most have a swing of about 10" (254mm) and a bed length of 12" to 14" (305mm to 356mm). The typical spindle is a 1" x 8 tpi, meaning it is 1" (25mm) in diameter, with 8 threads per inch. Mini-lathes do not have much distance between centers, but many now offer bed extensions to accommodate longer spindles. That makes them good for light-duty turning of furniture parts. A ½hp motor is virtually standard on a mini-lathe and most use a belt and stepped pulleys to provide multiple speeds. A few have a continuously variable speed control.

A mini-lathe is the right choice for true miniature work such as making dollhouse furniture, for a lathe dedicated to making pens, or for a machine you can carry to a vacation home or turning symposium.

For general woodturning, I believe mini-lathes fall short on a couple of fronts. The first is power. They will handle most small spindle work up to about 1½" (38mm) in diameter. If you want to turn larger bowls and vessels, though, I think you should avoid a mini-lathe. It may stall if you take aggressive cuts with large tools. Worse, the bearings for the headstock spindle may not be able to withstand the radial (across-axis) loads that are a necessary part of bowl turning. Unless you outfit the lathe with a bed extension, it will be too short to make useful furniture spindles.

A Brief History of the Lathe

The lathe is one of the oldest machines known to man. Exact first dating is impossible. The first lathes were probably spring pole or bow lathes, powered by the operator.

On a typical spring pole lathe, the bed consists of two stout timbers. A pair of poppets—large blocks of wood carrying a metal point center—is wedged in place on the bed. The centers hold the work in place.

A light rope was attached to a tree branch, either still on the tree or mounted above (or in some cases below) the lathe. The rope was wrapped around the work, and then tied to a long stick. Stepping on the stick makes the work spin several turns and bends the branch. At the bottom of the stroke, the branch pulls the rope back to the starting position, hence the name, *spring pole lathe*.

The bow lathe is another human-powered lathe. It uses a small longbow to power the lathe; the bowstring wraps around the work, which turns as the woodturner saws the bow back and forth. In India, Afghanistan, and Southeast Asia it is common, even today, to see workers using bow lathes on the ground, guiding the tools with their toes and left hand while they work the bow with their right hand.

Spring pole and bow lathes made faceplate bowl turning difficult because it was done between centers. Turning a bowl left a nubbin at the center; it would be broken away and the center smoothed with hand tools. In time, the left-hand poppet became a frame and supported a live, or driven, spindle—the headstock was born and with it the true, modern lathe. The development of the headstock also made faceplate turning easier and more practical.

The live spindle made possible the construction of the great wheel lathe. A pulley on the headstock spindle was belted to a wheel 4' to 6' (1,219mm to 1,829mm) in diameter, which an assistant turned.

By the nineteenth century, water and steam supplanted muscle power and the overhead shaft replaced the great wheel.

Medieval pole lathe. In the Middle Ages, woodturners roped the lathe to a springy pole or tree limb and used the pole's movement to turn the work. When the lathe went indoors, turners substituted a longbow for the pole.

Image courtesy Jan Van Vliet's Book of Crafts and Trades (1635).

Human power. A great wheel lathe, like this one at Colonial Williamsburg, runs on the massive flywheel, which is turned by hand.

A variation of the great wheel lathe was the treadle lathe, which drew its power from a foot treadle like the one on a sewing machine. Other designs used bicycle-like pedals. Both metal and ornamental treadle-powered lathes were common from the eighteenth century on.

In the twentieth century, the electric motor made possible lathes that could work anywhere. The last three decades have seen power inverters that make variable speed with little loss in power inexpensive.

The full-size lathe. A full-size lathe is big and powerful enough to handle just about any kind of turning you might want to try. Expect to pay at least $1,000 for a decent new lathe.

FULL-SIZE LATHES— ABOUT $1,000 AND UP

Full-size lathes are the best buy in the end if you are going to pursue turning to any degree. As a rule, they are heavier in construction, with substantial headstock, tailstock, banjo, and tool-rest castings. Most full-size lathes have a swing of 16" to 20" (406mm to 508mm), and a bed length of at least 30" (762mm), with the option to add bed extensions. (A couple of models have a smaller swing and shorter bed length.) Some full-size lathes have a 1¼" x 8 tpi (32 mm x 8) spindle, which is significantly more rigid than a 1 x 8tpi. A few have a 1½" x 8 tpi (38mm x 8) spindle, which is more rigid still. Also, the spindle bearings are designed to withstand the radial forces of bowl turning. Motors typically range from 1hp to 2hp, and a variable-speed control is common.

Whether you are a general woodworker who wants to add turning to your repertoire or want to do woodturning exclusively, one of the smaller full-sized lathes makes an excellent starting point. You get adequate swing and distance between centers to make almost any spindle you might need. A full-size lathe is also adequate for turning bowls.

If you ever want to turn something very large, such as a tabletop, a full-size lathe is your only choice. Some are designed for outboard turning, with a headstock that moves or rotates so that the workpiece hangs off the end or side of the lathe. Many older full-size lathes have threads on the outboard side of the spindle, which accommodate a faceplate.

Making Your Own Spring Pole Lathe

This spring pole lathe is adapted from plans given to me by Roy Underhill at the 2007 Williamsburg 18th Century Furniture Conference and used in his book, *The Woodwright's Guide: Working Wood with Wedge and Edge*. Roy drew his inspiration for this design from a drawing of a German lathe. I've made significant modifications to Roy's design to fit my taste and physique. Don't be afraid to do the same. I made the spindle the height of my elbow and raised the walking beam as high as possible, given the ceiling heights in the rooms where I use this beauty. I used white oak for all parts except the walking beam and movable poppit (tailstock), which are cherry. The only metal is the movable poppit spindle, its matching nut, and the lag screw that serves as the fixed poppit.

Materials List for Spring Pole Lathe

QUANTITY	COMPONENT	THICKNESS	WIDTH	LENGTH
1	Left Frame	1¼"	7"	47⅝"
1	Right Frame	1¼"	7"	80"
2	Trestles	1⅜"	3"	24"
1	Walking Beam	1"	2½"	65"
3	Rails	1¼"	4"	60"
1	Spring Pole	1⅛"	1⅛"	67"
1	Spring Pole	1⅛"	1⅛"	56"
6	Wedges	½"	1"	4"
1	Movable Poppit	4¾"	5⅞"	21"
2	Wedge	1¼"	3"	8"
1	Banjo	2"	3"	11⁹⁄₁₆"
1	Tool Rest Base	1¼"	4"	16"
1	Tool Rest	¾"	6⅞"	15"
1	Treadle Beam	¾"	2"	52"
1	Treadle Y	¾"	2"	30"
1	Treadle Base	¾"	2"	36"
2	Leather Strips			
1	Threaded Rod for spindle	¾"-16"		12⁹⁄₁₆"
1	Nut	¾"-16"		
1	Rope			
1	Lag Screw for Fixed Point	¾"		2"

A spring pole lathe in action. Every year, I give turning demonstrations at the local county fair, using a spring pole lathe.

Making Your Own Spring Pole Lathe *(continued)*

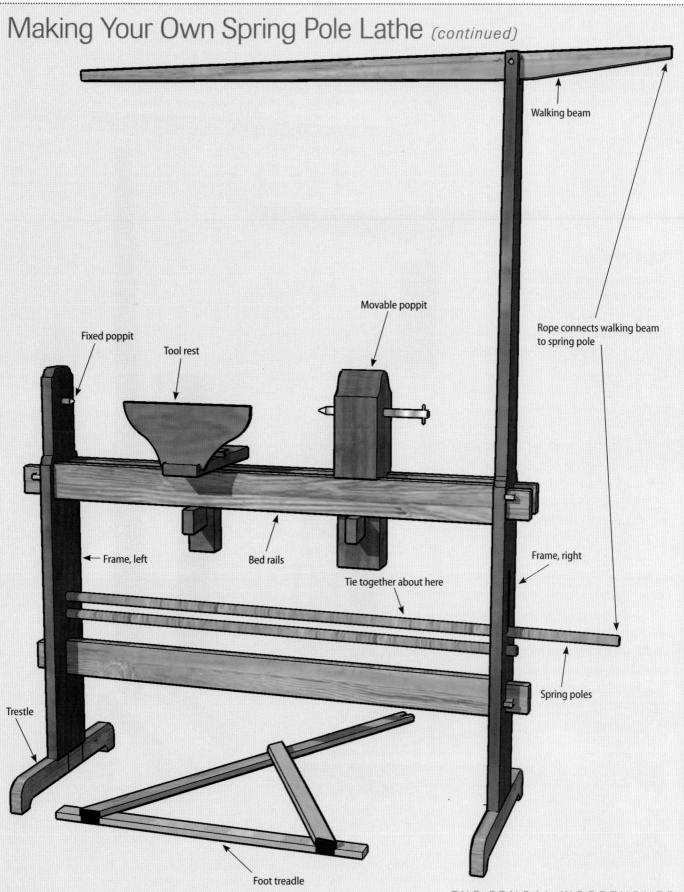

Walking beam

Movable poppit

Fixed poppit

Tool rest

Rope connects walking beam to spring pole

Frame, left

Bed rails

Frame, right

Tie together about here

Trestle

Spring poles

Foot treadle

Making Your Own Spring Pole Lathe *(continued)*

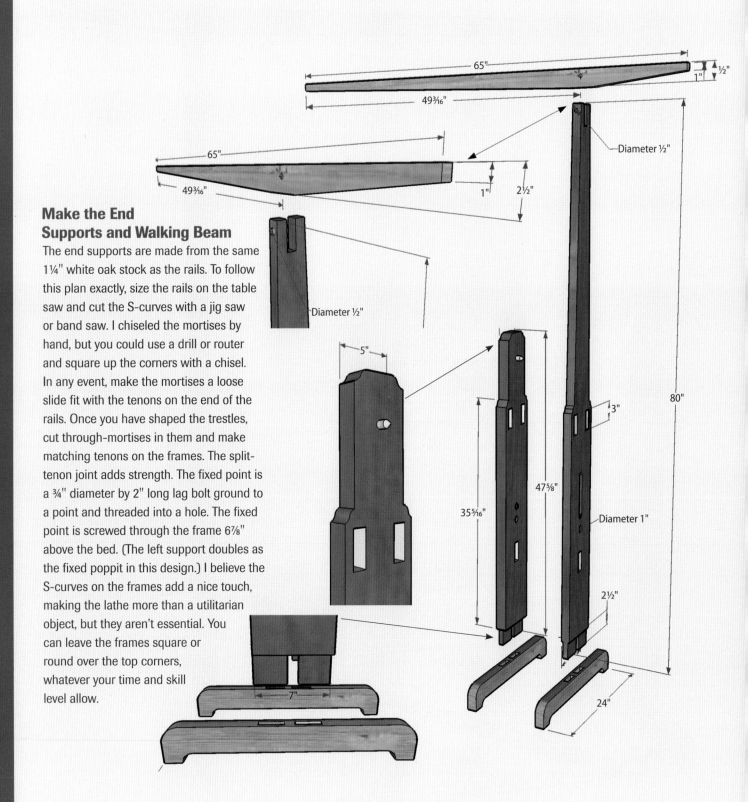

Make the End Supports and Walking Beam

The end supports are made from the same 1¼" white oak stock as the rails. To follow this plan exactly, size the rails on the table saw and cut the S-curves with a jig saw or band saw. I chiseled the mortises by hand, but you could use a drill or router and square up the corners with a chisel. In any event, make the mortises a loose slide fit with the tenons on the end of the rails. Once you have shaped the trestles, cut through-mortises in them and make matching tenons on the frames. The split-tenon joint adds strength. The fixed point is a ¾" diameter by 2" long lag bolt ground to a point and threaded into a hole. The fixed point is screwed through the frame 6⅞" above the bed. (The left support doubles as the fixed poppit in this design.) I believe the S-curves on the frames add a nice touch, making the lathe more than a utilitarian object, but they aren't essential. You can leave the frames square or round over the top corners, whatever your time and skill level allow.

Making Your Own Spring Pole Lathe *(continued)*

The Rails and Spring Poles

The 1¼" white oak rails are held in the frame with simple wedged mortise-and-tenon joints, which allow the lathe to be knocked down quickly for storage or transport. Cut the tenons with a band saw or by hand. On the top rails, the mortises for the wedges are staggered to make their removal easier. I cut the mortises with a hollow-chisel mortiser, tapering the holes with a chisel by hand. You can cut the mortises with a drill or router instead. Carve the spring poles with a drawknife and spokeshave, making them just over 1" in diameter at the center and just under 1" at the ends. To get the size right at the ends, use a block with a 1" diameter hole drilled in it as a gauge.

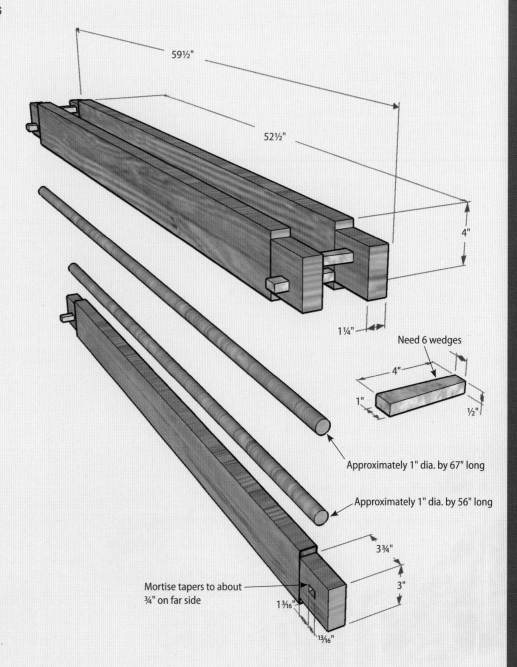

59½"

52½"

4"

1¼"

Need 6 wedges

4"

1"

½"

Approximately 1" dia. by 67" long

Approximately 1" dia. by 56" long

3¾"

3"

Mortise tapers to about ¾" on far side

1³⁄₁₆"

1³⁄₁₆"

CHAPTER

Making Your Own Spring Pole Lathe *(continued)*

The Movable Poppit

The Movable Poppit corresponds to the tailstock on a modern lathe. I made mine from a huge piece of cherry I'd been hoarding for years, but most people will have to make the blank by gluing together three pieces of thinner stock. Shape the curved top and cut the large tenon on the band saw. The centerpoint for the quill, or tailstock ram, is 6⅞" above the bed, to match the position of the fixed poppit point. Make the quill from a piece of ¾" x 16" threaded rod, which you can buy at a hardware store or home center. Bring the end to a point by spinning the rod against a grinder. Drill a clearance hole for the quill in the poppit, then chisel a pocket in the face to house the nut. Glue the nut in place with epoxy. Drill a ¼" hole through the quill for a ¼" by 2¼" long cross pin, which makes easy work of advancing and retracting of the quill.

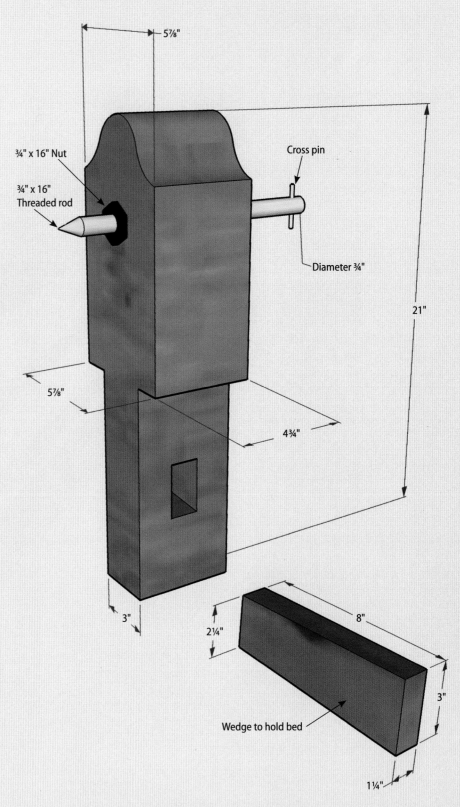

5⅞"

¾" x 16" Nut

¾" x 16" Threaded rod

Cross pin

Diameter ¾"

21"

5⅞"

4¾"

3"

2¼"

8"

3"

1¼"

Wedge to hold bed

Making Your Own Spring Pole Lathe *(continued)*

Tool Rest and Banjo

A wedged mortise-and-tenon joint holds the banjo in place and allows you to move it. The base of the tool rest is made from 1¼" thick white oak. I turned the round tenon on the banjo by chucking it between centers and chiseled the mortise by hand at the bench. I then drilled the hole for the cross pin and glued it in place.

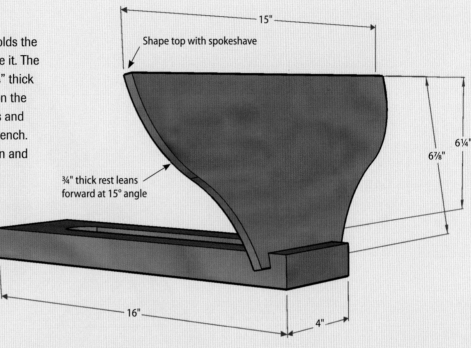

15"

Shape top with spokeshave

6¼"

6⅞"

¾" thick rest leans forward at 15° angle

16"

4"

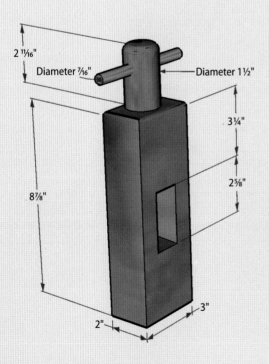

2 ¹¹⁄₁₆"

Diameter ⁷⁄₁₆"

Diameter 1½"

3¼"

2⅝"

8⅞"

2"

3"

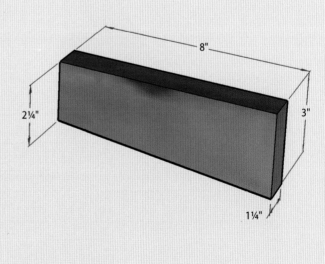

8"

2¼"

3"

1¼"

Making Your Own Spring Pole Lathe *(continued)*

Treadle

You can make the treadle from any available ¾" scrap stock. Screw or nail two pieces together at the crotch of the Y. Complete the treadle by tacking leather hinges in place.

The top spring pole is tied to the bottom. The further to the right the tie off is made, the stiffer and stronger the spring action. The right end of the top pole is then tied to the right end of the walking beam. At rest, the beam should be a bit higher on the left side. Now tie a rope to the left end of the walking beam, wrap it two to four times around the work, and tie it off in the hole of the treadle with a stopper knot, sometimes called a monkey's fist. At rest, the treadle should be slanted upward at about a 30° angle.

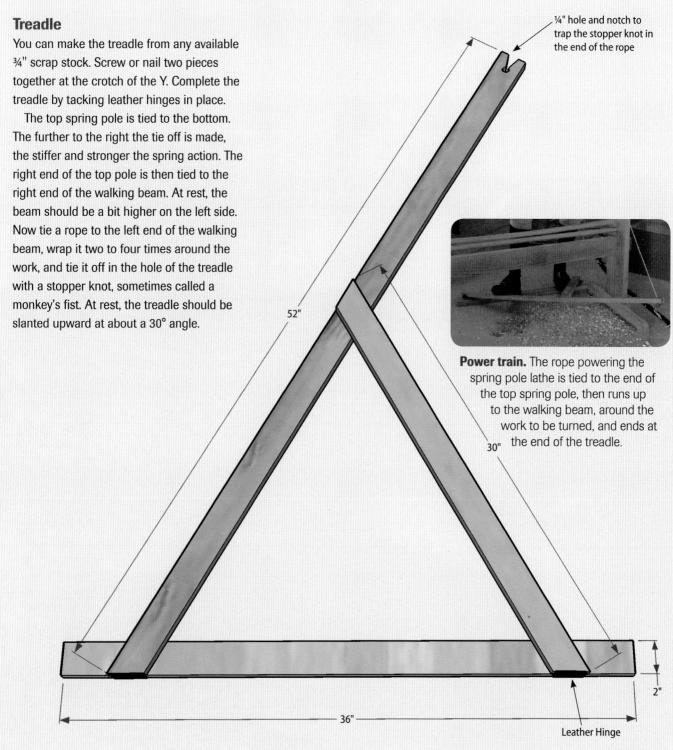

¼" hole and notch to trap the stopper knot in the end of the rope

52"

30"

36"

2"

Leather Hinge

Power train. The rope powering the spring pole lathe is tied to the end of the top spring pole, then runs up to the walking beam, around the work to be turned, and ends at the end of the treadle.

Sizing Up a Lathe, New or Used

While all lathes share the same basic pieces and parts, designs and manufacturing quality differ. Some manufacturers tout features that seem important but actually matter little to a serious woodturner. A good example is outboard turning. Almost all new lathe buyers worry inordinately about this feature, but most will never use it.

I consider used equipment to be the best value. My father and I have always been champions of previously owned machinery, both for our machine shop and for our private use. The following sections cover what I have learned about judging a lathe. This information will empower you to become a perceptive buyer, whether you are buying new or used.

THE BED

A lathe bed is typically made from cast iron or structural steel. One manufacturer offers a mini-lathe with a bed and headstock made from black granite. The bed supports the headstock, tailstock, and banjo. The ways are the flat, polished surfaces of the bed, which allow the banjo and tailstock to move freely.

Cast iron is a good, time-honored material. It is heavy but not very stiff, and so dampens vibration well.

Structural steel is much stiffer. Unless the manufacturer places welds at strategic spots to keep vibrations from resonating and multiplying, steel transmits them like a tuning fork. A badly designed structural steel lathe is no fun to use; however, a well-designed one is a joy.

The worst bed material, I believe, is tubing or solid round bar stock. It is too flexible and transmits annoying amounts of vibration.

If you are considering a used lathe, the main thing to look for in the bed is mass, vibration-damping, and enough length between centers to suit you. A test run should quickly tell you whether the lathe meets your needs.

A used lathe may have a twisted bed, the result of the lathe not being level. You can check for that condition and correct it by placing a good level at several points across the bed. Adjust one or more of the contact points with the floor until you get the same level reading everywhere on the bed.

Lathe Spindle

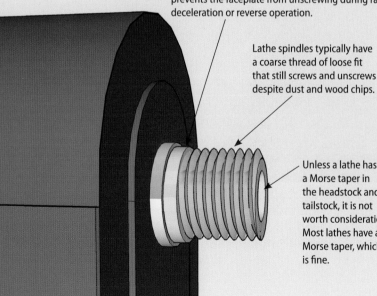

Some spindles have a shoulder area designers incorporate to center a specially counterbored faceplate. The shoulder area also provides an area for engagement of a locking grub screw in specially designed faceplates. Tightening the grub screw prevents the faceplate from unscrewing during rapid deceleration or reverse operation.

Lathe spindles typically have a coarse thread of loose fit that still screws and unscrews despite dust and wood chips.

Unless a lathe has a Morse taper in the headstock and tailstock, it is not worth consideration. Most lathes have a #2 Morse taper, which is fine.

THE HEADSTOCK

The most important parts of the headstock are the spindle and the bearings that allow it to spin. Spindle turning does not place great demands on the headstock because almost all of the force consists of pressure between the centers. A small spindle in decent ball bearings will be completely adequate. For work mounted on a faceplate, however, you need bearings that are free of play and designed to handle both radial (sidewise) and axial (lengthwise) loads. Bearing size and quality tend to increase with spindle size. A lathe's spindle size is fixed and can't be changed.

A common spindle diameter, especially in older lathes, is 1" (25mm), because Delta Tool Company years ago created a de facto industry standard with the 1" x 8 tpi spindle configuration. Unfortunately, that size lacks enough stiffness for serious bowl work in green wood. It tends to flex or vibrate when holding a faceplate laden with a big, heavy bowl blank. For bowl turning or heavy spindle turning, you are better off choosing a lathe with a spindle diameter of 1⅛" (29mm) or larger.

A thicker spindle is stiffer and better able to withstand radial loads. That is because the stiffness of the round bar that makes up the spindle increases by a power of four with the diameter. Even a small increase, as from 1" to 1¾" (25mm to 32mm), increases stiffness by 60%. See the table above right.

The center of the headstock spindle is fitted with a Morse taper. This American innovation, dating from the time of the Industrial Revolution, is a sure, trouble-free way to mount accessories such as the drive center that holds a spindle to be turned. A Morse taper is a locking taper—once the accessory snaps into the tapered hole, it locks in place.

Spindle Size and Stiffness

As you increase the diameter of a spindle, its stiffness increases greatly.

SPINDLE SIZE	STIFFNESS FACTOR	COMMENT
1" (25 mm)	1	Suitable for light duty turning
1⅛" (29 mm)	1.6	Suitable for small bowl turning
1¼" (32mm)	2.4	Suitable for heavy bowls or thick spindles
1½" (38mm)	5.1	The sky is the limit

The business end of a lathe. The threads on the headstock spindle accept many of the chucks that hold the work in place. A Morse taper shapes the middle of the spindle, which holds various accessories. The greater the spindle diameter, the stiffer it is.

A selection of centers. All of the accessories shown here have a Morse taper, which fits into a matching taper in the headstock spindle and the tailstock.

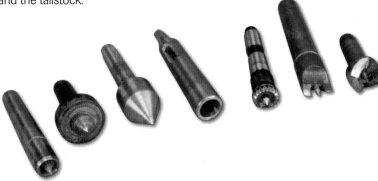

Morse Taper Sizes

SIZE	DIAMETER, SMALL END	DIAMETER, LARGE END	LENGTH
0	.252" (6mm)	.356" (9mm)	2¹¹⁄₃₂" (59.5mm)
1	.369" (9mm)	.475" (12mm)	2⁹⁄₁₆" (65mm)
2	.572" (14.5mm)	.700" (18mm)	3⅛" (79mm)
3	.778" (20mm)	.938" (24mm)	3⅞" (98mm)

Morse taper adapter. An adapter like the one shown here lets you fit a smaller Morse taper accessory into a larger socket. Using an adapter means you do not have to buy a full set of new accessories if you buy a new lathe with a larger Morse taper.

Lathe spindles typically have Morse tapers ranging from #0 to #3, with #2 being the most common. (As the chart on the left shows, the numbers designate different sizes.) The accessory and the tapered hole must have the same taper if the accessory is to fit tightly. However, you can buy an adapter such as the one at left, which will allow you to fit a small accessory in a large taper.

To check the condition of a Morse taper on a used lathe, shine a light into the socket and look for scoring left behind by a drive center or a drill chuck. Such scoring is not necessarily a reason to reject the lathe, but it means you will need to sand the taper smooth or re-ream it.

To sand the taper, cut a slot in a dowel, insert the end of a piece of 150-grit emery paper in the slot, and wrap it around the dowel. Put the dowel in the spindle socket and twist it to sand out the taper. Doing it manually is possible but slow. I have turned the dowel in an electric drill to good effect, and even powered up the lathe to quickly clean up a headstock spindle.

To re-ream a Morse taper socket, you will need to buy a reamer from a machine-tool supply house. The reamer can be fitted into a drill chuck and mounted in the tailstock or headstock to ream the opposing spindle. With the lathe unplugged and the reamer mounted in the appropriate spindle, put some machine oil on it and slide it into the opposing spindle until you feel contact. Now turn the headstock by hand while keeping light pressure on the reamer. Use a wrench to prevent the reamer from turning. The result is a socket that is good as new. You can even use a reamer to straighten out a socket that is bored off-axis.

Early lathes used plain bearings. White metal rings, cast in an alloy known as Babbitt, supported a raised rib on the spindle, called a *journal*. A plain bearing will run forever if kept well lubricated, but it will fail quickly if allowed to run dry. You may find used lathes with plain bearings. You can usually identify plain bearing lathes because they have two oiling holes, or *cups*, on the top of the headstock. Unless the bearings feel tight when you turn the spindle by hand, you would best avoid the lathe.

An advance from the plain bearing was the rolling element bearing. The most common is the ball bearing, which is responsible for today's trouble-free and maintenance-free lathes. Larger spindles require larger bearings. Larger bearings, or bearings spaced farther apart, are better able to take the heavier radial loads of bowl turning.

Ball bearings can be replaced without too much trouble. So even if the ball bearings in a used lathe are shot, the lathe may be worth buying. The bearings are generally a press fit with the spindle journals. They may be a press fit with the headstock casting as well, or they may be held with snap rings. I have often pushed bearings out of machinery using wood blocks I turned in a lathe and the tail vise in my European workbench. An automotive repair shop will often do the job for you at reasonable cost.

POWER AND DRIVE MECHANISMS

The speed of a modern lathe is controlled in one of four ways.

Simple AC motor and stepped pulleys. Normal motors run at a fixed speed and horsepower. The simplest way to get multiple speeds is to run a belt between the motor and the lathe spindle and use pulleys (also called sheaves) of varying diameters. Most lathes with this type of basic speed control have four or more sheaves that yield a speed range of 500 rpm to 2,800 rpm, with each step up increasing the speed by a few hundred rpm.

Reeves drive. This is a time-honored variable-speed system that uses variable-width sheaves split down the middle. It is traditionally the least expensive variable-speed system. A lever near the headstock controls the width of the driving sheave while a spring keeps the driven sheave tight on the belt and takes slack out of the system. Moving the halves of the driving sheave further apart decreases the effective diameter, for the belt rides lower in the sheave.

Don't Obsess Over Speed

It is important, especially in faceplate turning, not to begin with the lathe running too fast. The work could fly off and hurt you. That said, in most instances you only want to go faster or slower, rather than nail a precise speed. Exact rpm is something only new turners seem to worry greatly about.

I cannot remember the last time I consulted the speed chart on any of my lathes. I know from experience that such-and-such a job will take a particular belt-and-pulley combination or a specific speed-dial setting. I do not look at the numbers but rather just go faster or slower as the job dictates.

Variable speed is a great luxury, because with it you can often eliminate vibration by going a few rpm faster or slower. It is also beneficial to slow down the lathe when you are using a skew chisel.

Speed steps. Found on most mini-lathes and a few full-size models, multiple pulleys are the simplest, cheapest form of speed control. To change speeds, just move the belt from one pulley to another. You can also add a variable-speed motor; the pulleys act like an automobile transmission and the motor like the accelerator.

The spring-loaded drive sheave (on the spindle) adjusts automatically and the lathe goes slower. Moving the lever the other way pushes the sheaves closer together, increasing the diameter, so the lathe goes faster. Reeves drives suffer from high belt wear and tear. Replacing a belt now and then is no big deal, though. There are huge numbers of used lathes on the market that have a Reeves drive.

Direct-current motor. The direct-current (DC) motor is well suited for powering a lathe because varying the voltage also controls the speed. The advent of solid-state electronics in the late-twentieth century has made it possible to design small controllers that deliver varying voltage DC power. Most variable-speed mini-lathes and bench-top lathes use DC motors and controllers. Edison believed in direct current as I do.

AC inverters with three-phase motor. Varying the voltage to an AC motor won't change the speed—it will just burn it up. The speed is controlled by the cycle rate of the alternating current. North America and Japan have adopted 60-cycle standards, so motors there run at either 1,725 rpm or 3,300 rpm. Those speeds are a function of the cycle rate of the electrical current that makes a three-phase induction motor run. Europe and many other parts of the world use 50-cycle AC current, which yields speeds that are five-sixths those of 60-cycle current: 1,438 rpm instead of 1,725, for example.

An inverter makes it easy to change the current's cycle rate, producing a nifty speed-control device that you'll find on many full-size lathes. An AC inverter is my favorite speed-control method because it allows very quick and seamless speed changes. DC power is close behind.

The usual scheme is to install a three-phase motor on the lathe and pair it with an inverter, which doubles the cycle rate of the available current. That yields 120 cycles in North America. This also nearly doubles the horsepower, giving the motor robust power at high speeds. Most inverters will produce cycle rates as low as 2, giving low speed with nearly all the rated horsepower.

A solid-state inverter is probably the best way to control speed on a lathe today. It is also a great retrofit to an older lathe. You can buy a three-phase motor for as little as $25 per horsepower and an inverter for $100 to $135 or so.

BELTS

Most lathes use V-belts or poly V-belts. V-belts do not slip the way flat belts can, but they are prone to slight amounts of surging. The slight speed fluctuations are seldom of much consequence in woodturning, however.

Many manufacturers are turning to poly-V belts, which have a series of very small V-shaped ribs molded into the inside of a flat neoprene belt. The sheaves have corresponding V-grooves machined into them. The result is a positive drive system without slips or surges. In addition, poly-V-belts last much longer than V-belts. They do require much higher belt tension, however.

It is important for the belt to have adequate cross-section and area to transmit power from the motor to the workpiece. Top-of-the-line lathes have belts that are larger than necessary, while economy lathes often get some of that economy with a scrawny belt.

Electronic speed control. Found mainly on full-size lathes, as well as a few mini-lathes, an electronic control delivers smooth, instantaneous speed changes as you turn a knob.

SWING

Swing is the diameter of work that can be accommodated over the bed and is twice the distance from the top of the bed to the center of the spindle.

It's a highly touted figure but can be misleading. For spindle turning and nearly all bowl work, the nominal swing is diminished by twice the height of the banjo, which must fit under the spinning work. Two lathes with the same advertised swing might have very different banjo heights and thus very different actual swings. Good lathe design tries to keep the height of the banjo as low as possible. To find the actual swing of your lathe, park the banjo under the spindle nose and measure the distance from the top of the banjo to the center of the spindle. Double that measurement (the measurement is half the swing).

INDEXING

Indexing lets you lock the headstock spindle at precisely defined points so you can carry out secondary operations, such as reeding and fluting of furniture legs or architectural columns. It can also be useful for carving flutes on bowls. Most indexing heads have 24 stops, but you can find lathes with as few as 12 indexing stops or as many as 60.

Indexing is something that concerns new lathe buyers greatly, even though only a small percentage of turners use the feature. What's more, there are many ways to lay out regular spacing for flutes, reeds, or carving on the odd project.

Particularly easy is 4 spacings, which entails using the layout lines drawn between the corners of a square billet. Equally simple are 3 or 6 spacings, which can be found by picking up the diameter or radius of the workpiece with dividers and walking them around the circumference. For a one-time project, you can find almost any number of spacings with dividers by trial and error. If you want to be more precise, see *An All-Purpose Indexing Method*, on page 32.

It may be tempting to use the indexing feature to lock the spindle when removing a chuck or faceplate. That is not a good idea because you might shear off the indexing pin. It is better to use the dedicated spindle lock found on some lathes, or the wrench or tommy bar supplied with others.

An All-Purpose Indexing Method

Here is how to divide a circle or cylinder of any size into any number of segments.

Mark the Work. Wrap a piece of masking tape around the piece you want to divide and mark where the two ends meet. Straighten out the tape and stick it flush with the edge of your bench; tape down some paper above it.

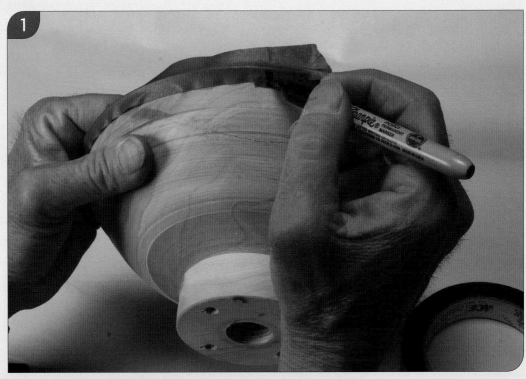

Divide the distance. Use a square to extend vertical lines from the pair of marks. Measure that distance and pick a larger but easily divisible number. For example, if the circumference is 28" (711mm) and you want to divide that into 10 segments, pick 30" (762mm). Angle a ruler across the paper so that 0 is on one vertical and 30 is on the other. Make a tick mark on the paper every 3" (76mm). Use a square to transfer each of these tick marks back down to the tape. Wrap the tape around the workpiece and transfer the marks to it.

TOOL REST & BANJO

What we commonly call a tool rest actually consists of two parts. The first is the T-shaped rest that supports the turning tools, and the second is the banjo that supports it. The banjo has two locking mechanisms. The first holds the tool rest securely at any height and angle you desire, while the second holds the banjo itself fast to the bed.

The banjo must be moved often during turning, so its clamping mechanism must keep the tool base securely locked to the bed yet allow you to move it quickly and easily as needed. The tool-rest clamping mechanism must hold the longest of tool rests securely with a tool perched on the very end, even during heavy roughing. And the banjo

A well-shaped tool rest. A good tool rest angles to create a fulcrum point for tools. A tool rest rounded at the top will not provide good support.

must be long enough to accommodate the lathe's maximum swing. To check this, slide the banjo as far toward you as it will go and lock the tool rest parallel to the lathe bed. Now see whether the tool rest clears the largest swing.

Entry-level lathes (including most mini-lathes) come with a tool rest that is either too short to be useful or poorly shaped. You can buy replacement tool rests from retailers such as Woodcraft (*www.woodcraft.com*), BestWood Tools (*http://bestwoodtools.stores.yahoo.net*), and Penn State Industries (*www.pennstateind.com*). Woodcraft and BestWood Tools sell tool rests with interchangeable posts usable on different lathes—you just buy a new post if you buy a bigger or smaller lathe. Some of the systems use a round bar for the rest, which is fine for bowl turning, but less than ideal for spindle turning.

The tool rest itself is a fulcrum point between the handle and the cutting edge of the turning tool. In order for the tool to slide easily along the rest, the fulcrum point must be a small area, usually a small-radius knife-edge. A well-designed tool rest will have a front edge that slopes away from the fulcrum edge at an acute angle. Most spindle tools are ground with a bevel of 25° to 30°, so the tool will be held at that angle or greater during turning. If the tool rest has the proper slope, you can place the fulcrum point close to the work and it will provide good leverage. Many rests I have seen are rather round in design, which means that for certain types of cuts the tool will not be on the fulcrum edge. That can make for dicey tool handling. If your rest suffers from that shortcoming, you can usually file it to the proper profile.

The Tool Rest

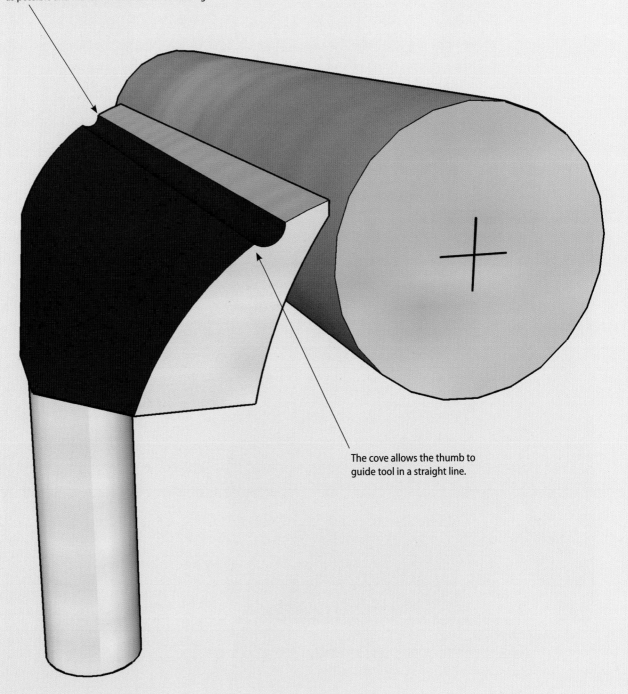

Good tool rest design has sufficient slope behind the fulcrum edge. This puts the support for the tool as close to the turning as possible and makes for the best tool handling.

The cove allows the thumb to guide tool in a straight line.

TAILSTOCK

Few lathe buyers consider the tailstock when buying a lathe, but they should. In fact, faceplate turners, especially those specializing in large bowls, often believe they do not even need a tailstock. That is shortsighted, because the tailstock is handy in many ways. By bringing it up against newly mounted work, it removes much of the strain on the faceplate or chuck, providing a tremendous margin of safety when you begin roughing out a bowl. There are also any number of nifty faceplate turning tricks and chucking methods that entail the use of the tailstock. I will describe some of the more useful ones in Chapter 5.

The tailstock is composed of the main casting, the spindle, the hand wheel, and a clamping mechanism that holds the entire assembly in place on the bed. The tailstock should be heavy, in proportion to the lathe. The spindle, or quill, should be equipped with a Morse taper (my choice is #2 or larger). The spindle should be thick enough to secure the work without bending or deflecting—¾" (19 mm) diameter is minimum; 1" (25mm) or larger is better. There should be plenty of spindle travel—the more the better. A minimum is 2½" (64mm). The tailstock should lock fast to the bed and not move during turning.

Steadying long spindles. If you are going to turn many flag poles, it is worth getting a commercial steady rest such as this Oneway, which I have found to be the best available. It mounts on any lathe, even a classic Conover with a wood bed.

Most tailstocks have a handwheel to move the spindles. Some older machines sometimes have a lever-operated spindle that can be tightened with a hand wheel. That is well suited for production spindle turning or metal spinning because you can easily move a workpiece on or off the lathe.

Many tailstock spindles have a self-ejecting feature that spits the Morse taper out of the spindle when it is fully retracted. You would do that whenever you change from a live center to, say, a drill chuck to hold a drill bit. Instead, some lathes have a hollow tailstock spindle, which allows you to run a drill through the tailstock instead of mounting a drill chuck.

When purchasing a lathe, be sure the tailstock aligns with the headstock. Put centers that come to a point in each end, and then slide the tailstock up until the two centers touch. Ideally, the two points will touch exactly. A misalignment is of no consequence in spindle turning, because the work must only be true to itself. Exact center alignment is most important for faceplate work, where operations like drilling must be done precisely on center.

THE STAND

My father would have said, "You do not put a Rolex watch in a brass case." Likewise, you do not want to perch a fine lathe on a rickety stand. A stand has to be solid, have a good footprint, inhibit vibration, and have all four legs make equally good contact with the floor.

Solid means that the stand will not rock under side loading—the kind of load it sustains when you push a turning tool against the work. A good footprint means the stand will resist tipping but let you stand close without having your feet hitting the legs. Wedges or leveling bolts give the legs solid contact with the floor and allow you to undo any twisting from the bed.

Inhibiting vibration is the most difficult aspect of lathe-stand design. I believe enclosed sheet-metal stands are the worst. They tend to exacerbate noise and vibration. A fair number of modern stands are cast iron or tubular or angular structural steel and tend to work out well because they add plenty of mass and are designed to dampen vibration.

Conclusion

The perfect lathe is the topic of great debate. No two turners agree on what is right. We tend to favor what we grew up with or what is familiar. What is familiar is largely a matter of who trained us, so to a certain extent, we are all victims of the predispositions of our mentors. If you keep an open mind, you will find a range of lathes that will allow you to produce fine work. It is virtually impossible to find a lathe with all of the features you want. You will have to make some compromises or modify the equipment. That is why my father and I designed our own lathe. (The spindle height was bang-on for us). I have seen many fine turners work with all manner of cobbled-together systems. You may well be the most important component of your lathe—the extra nut behind the hand wheel.

Building a Shopmade Lathe Stand

You can make your own sturdy, stable lathe stand for much less than the cost of a commercial one. It is often useful to weight it with sand, which dampens vibration and prevents it from rocking.

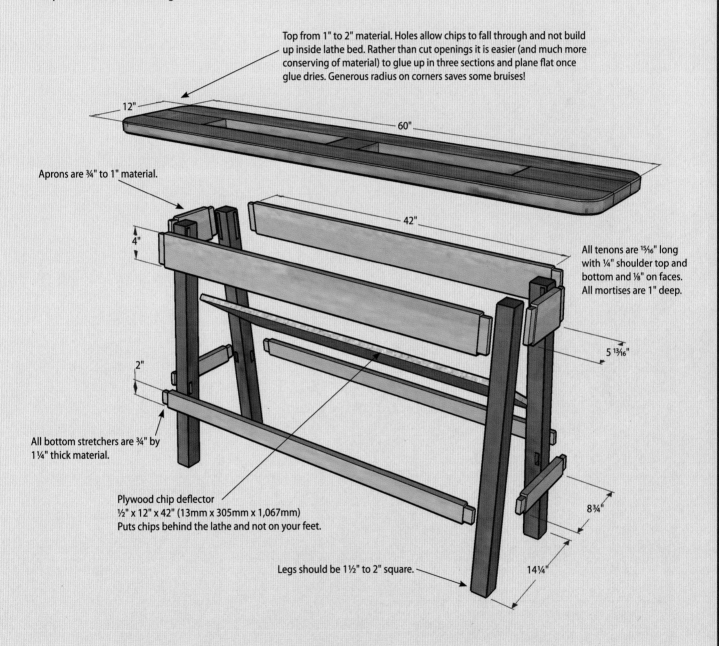

Top from 1" to 2" material. Holes allow chips to fall through and not build up inside lathe bed. Rather than cut openings it is easier (and much more conserving of material) to glue up in three sections and plane flat once glue dries. Generous radius on corners saves some bruises!

12"

60"

Aprons are ¾" to 1" material.

42"

4"

All tenons are ¹⁵⁄₁₆" long with ¼" shoulder top and bottom and ⅛" on faces. All mortises are 1" deep.

5 ¹³⁄₁₆"

2"

All bottom stretchers are ¾" by 1¼" thick material.

Plywood chip deflector
½" x 12" x 42" (13mm x 305mm x 1,067mm)
Puts chips behind the lathe and not on your feet.

8¾"

Legs should be 1½" to 2" square.

14¼"

Finding Good Tools Without Breaking the Bank

2

After the lathe, tools are a woodturner's second necessity. Fortunately, you do not have to buy all your turning tools at once. The most economical approach involves following a short list of advisories:

- **Buy enough tools** to get started, adding more as the need arises and your budget allows.
- **Avoid purchasing** prepackaged sets of tools, which are usually a bad value. The sets invariably contain tools that are the wrong size for a beginner or just not useful.
- **Be daring:** fashion your own scrapers and other tools from steel destined for the scrap heap.

In this chapter, I will sort out the various types of turning tools and explain whether you do or do not need each one. I will explain what tools are easy to find on the used market and how to discern good ones from bad. I will also show you how to make scrapers from old files and other pieces of discarded metal.

Many tools can be improvised or found on the used tool market, while others are best purchased new. From left to right, the first tool is an improvised scraper for hollow spindle turning made from a screwdriver. The second is an improvised chatter tool. The next is a classic Sears skew chisel followed by a parting tool, both of which tend to be serviceable hand-me-downs. Next is a classic Buck Brothers spindle gouge made in the very early twentieth century. The last tool is a Doug Thompson detail gouge, for which I made my own handle; it is my favorite spindle gouge.

The Three Families of Turning Tools

Woodturning tools fall into three broad categories: gouges, chisels, and scrapers.

There are several types of gouges, each designed for a specific task, such as shaping a bowl or transforming a square length of wood into a cylinder. Whatever its function, a gouge resembles a chisel rolled into a half-cylinder. The hollowed-out part of the cylinder is called the flute. A gouge's single-bevel cutting edge rides against the work to cut, much the way a plane iron cuts as it slides across the flat face of a board.

Chisels include the skew chisel, the parting (or cutoff) tool, the beading and parting tool, and the bedan. They are relatively difficult to use, but if handled correctly, they leave the best surface finish. Chisels are generally used for spindle work. With the exception of the bedan, a fairly specialized tool used only for shaping tenons, woodturning chisels are double-bevel tools. The two bevels form the cutting edge.

Scrapers are used with the edge dragging against the wood. When you sharpen a scraper, you leave the edge with a burr that does the cutting. Unlike other turning tools, which are used level or pointed uphill on the tool rest, scrapers point downhill so the edge drags and the burr cuts.

If you are buying new turning gouges or chisels, I recommend buying ones made of high-speed steel (HSS). They are most affordable and offer the best long-term value because they hold their edge well and are immune from burning in the grinder. Tools made from powdered metal are widely available, and manufacturers claim that powdered metal tools hold an edge much longer than their HSS counterparts, making them seem a great value. But I think HSS tools actually offer the best bang for the buck for beginners.

Woodturners Refer to The Length of the Bevel, Not the Specific Angle of Grind

The angle of grind on turning tools can be confusing for two reasons. First, turners tend to refer to the length of a grind rather than a specific angle. Second, people sometimes cite an angle that refers to the metal ground away, not to the angle left on the tool after grinding.

To minimize confusion in this book, a bevel angle always refers to the angle on the tool itself. Think of a short grind as 70°, a medium grind as 45° to 50°, and a long grind as 25° to 30°.

In spindle turning, you are always cutting directly across the grain so a long, or acute, cutting angle works best—something on the order of 25° to 30° at the nose of a spindle gouge.

In faceplate work, you cut dead against the grain twice a revolution. A long grind will make a gouge just dig in and catch. Therefore, grind bowl gouges to medium angles—between 40°

and 50°—at their sides, where they do most of their work. They are ground even blunter on the nose. Typical nose grinds for a bowl gouge are about 70°.

Scrapers are ground short, to about 75°. Chisels have a long to medium grind, between 22° and 42°.

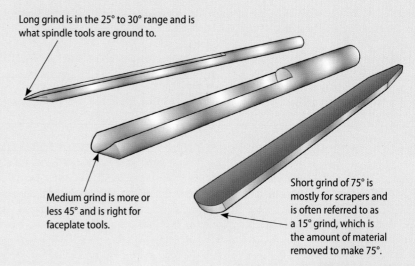

Long grind is in the 25° to 30° range and is what spindle tools are ground to.

Medium grind is more or less 45° and is right for faceplate tools.

Short grind of 75° is mostly for scrapers and is often referred to as a 15° grind, which is the amount of material removed to make 75°.

Three Families of Turning Tools

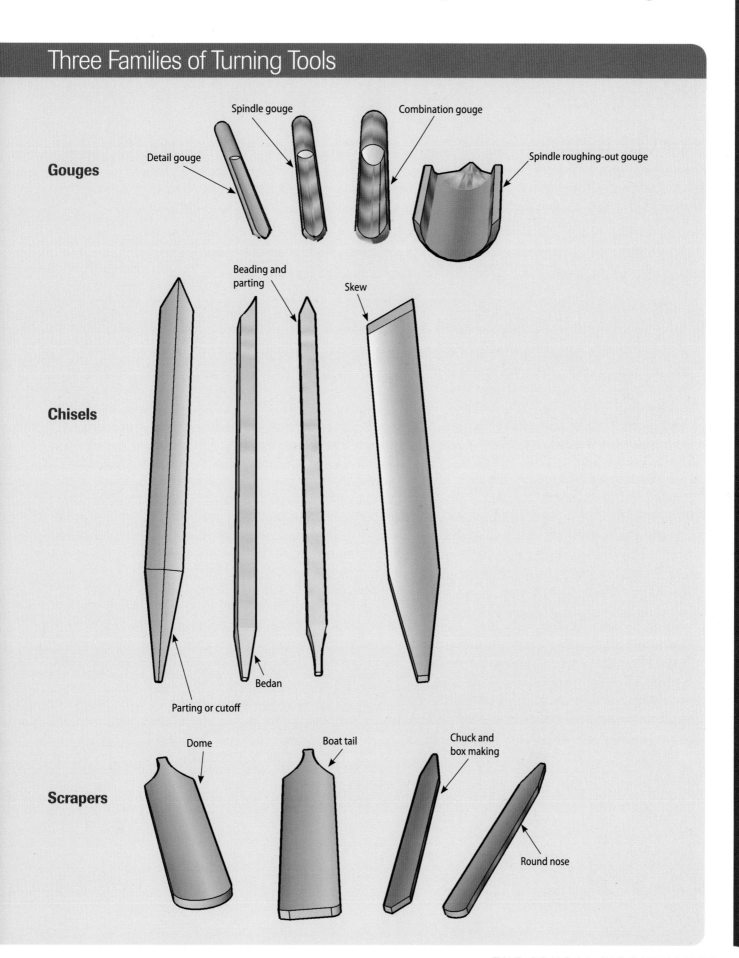

Gouges

Detail gouge

Spindle gouge

Combination gouge

Spindle roughing-out gouge

Chisels

Beading and parting

Skew

Parting or cutoff

Bedan

Scrapers

Dome

Boat tail

Chuck and box making

Round nose

Tools for Spindle Turning

SPINDLE GOUGE

The spindle gouge is probably the most difficult tool to buy for several reasons.

The first reason is it always comes from the factory ground too short, and sometimes not even the correct shape. You can pay a lot of money for a badly ground spindle gouge.

The second reason is the shape of the flute. It is always a radius of a circle, but it should be shallow enough for the tool to take a long fingernail grind. (Shallow-flute gouges are sometimes called *detail gouges*.) A deeper flute cannot be ground as long, and will not make superior spindle cuts.

A Short Course in Steelmaking

Woodworking tools are made from tool steel, an alloy of iron and carbon. Perfect tool steel would be hard (able to hold an edge) and tough (able to resist shock without breaking.) Unfortunately, hardness and toughness are mutually exclusive qualities. Hard steel lacks toughness, while tough steel lacks hardness.

In 1914, Hugh M. and Stanley P. Rockwell developed the Rockwell Scale, the standard measure of steel hardness. The Rockwell C scale measures tool steel's hardness by checking the penetration of a 120° diamond cone when applying a 150-kilogram load. The test leaves only a small pit in the sample. The table gives the relevant numbers.

High-carbon steel, which holds an edge well, contains between 0.8% and 1.5% carbon. To harden high-carbon steel, it is heated to about 1,600° F, then plunged into water or brine. This brings the metal to full hardness, RHC 64 to 68 on the Rockwell Scale. The metal is now tempered by being heated again to a lower temperature, bringing the hardness back to what the toolmaker has decided will give the best balance between hardness and toughness.

Modern steel formulas

Starting in the nineteenth century, steelmakers began adding other elements to steel to give it other useful properties. Vanadium, for instance, increases the ability to hold an edge. Manganese slows the critical rate of cooling, allowing cooling in oil rather than water. (The "O" in O1 steel stands for oil.)

In 1868, Robert Mushet developed steel with 7% tungsten content, now considered the forerunner of modern high-speed steel. At the end of the nineteenth century, Frederick Taylor and Maunsel White headed a Bethlehem Steel team that perfected modern high-speed steel by alloying tungsten and heat-treating at higher temperatures.

In the last two decades, metallurgists have developed powdered metal steel, which contains up to 15% vanadium, greatly increasing the working life of an edge. In conventional steelmaking, more than about 2% vanadium causes strings of vanadium carbide to form, making it impossible to machine the metal. Powdered metal technology mechanically mixes the metals in powdered form, and then sprays the alloy into a furnace so it becomes plastic, not molten.

NORMAL HARDNESS OF VARIOUS TOOLS	
Fully-Hardened High-Carbon Steel	HRC 68
Japanese Tools	HRC 64 – 65
Bench Chisels, Plane Blades, Turning Chisels and Gouges	HRC 58 – 62
Scrapers, Mortise Chisels, Springs	HRC 48 – 51
Axes, Cold Chisels	HRC 40 – 45
Fully Annealed Steel	HRC 20

Spindle Gouges

The flute in a spindle gouge is always a radius of a circle, but can be shallow or deep. The depth of the flute controls how sharp the angle of the cutting edge is.

Detail

Normal spindle

Combination

The shallower the flute on a spindle gouge, the longer the grind and the sharper the fingernail cutting edge you can obtain. That is why I like the detail gouge—it can be ground to a very long fingernail.

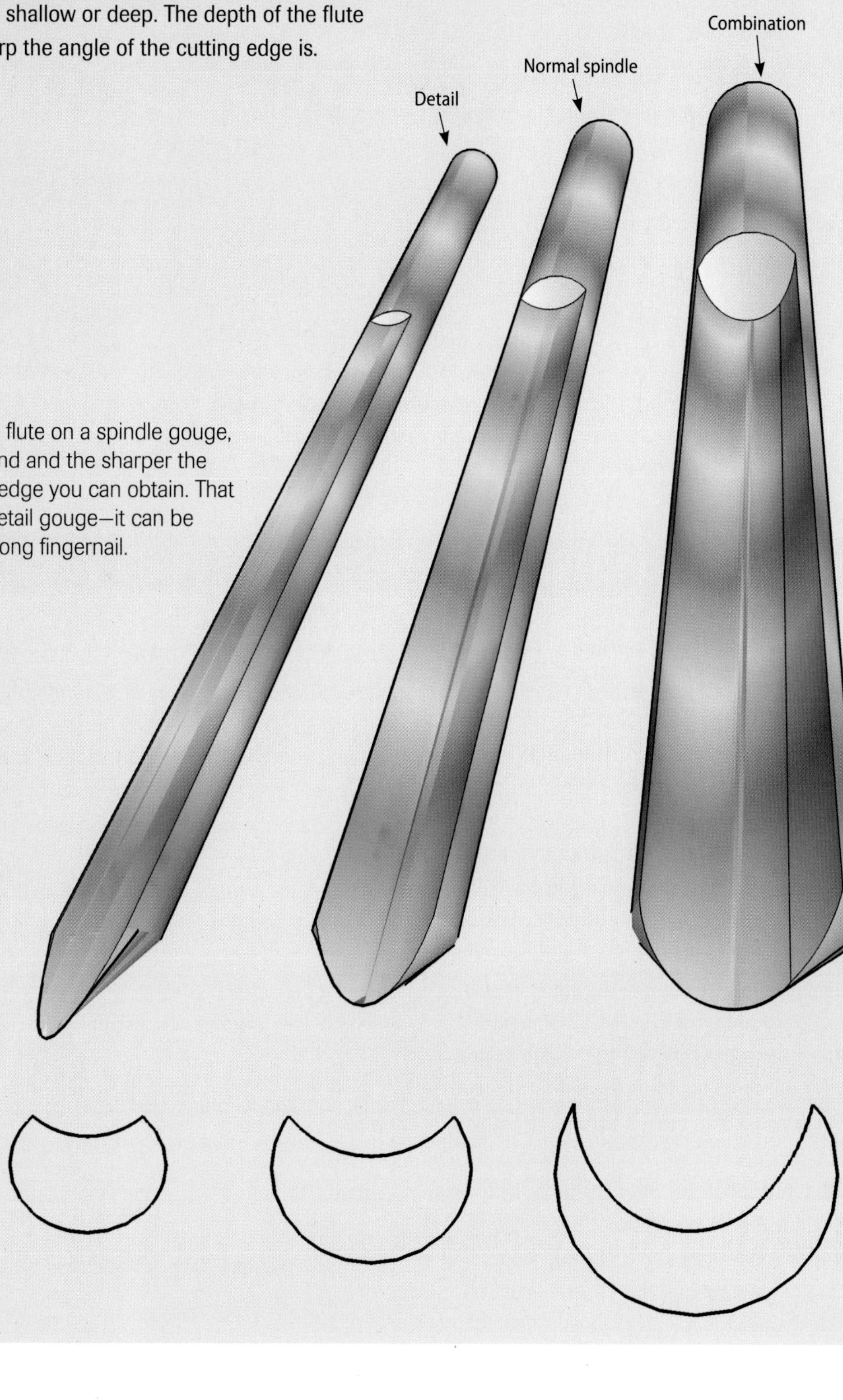

Third is the tool size. The traditional way to size a gouge refers to distance across the flute. However, some manufacturers refer to the diameter of the bar the gouge is made from. In this book, gouge sizes always mean the distance across the flute.

A ½" (13mm) gouge is a good starting size and will do the bulk of everyday spindle turning. Avoid any spindle gouge smaller than about ⅜" (10mm) because it will not have adequate stiffness. A ¼" (6mm) spindle gouge is wiggly and next to useless.

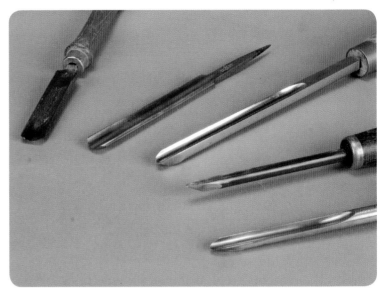

A selection of spindle gouges. Older spindle gouges, like the two at left, were forged from flat pieces of steel. Newer gouges have the flute ground into a bar. They also have their cutting edge ground to a sharp angle, known as a fingernail grind.

Is Powdered Metal Really a Bargain?

Recent independent tests have shown something I have long suspected. Powdered metal tools have a much longer life for metal cutting, but not for cutting wood. One manufacturer claims that its ProPM powdered-metal ½" (13mm) bowl gouge has three times the edge life of the same size gouge in M2 high-speed steel (HSS).

However, the study *Ranking Wear Resistance of Tool Steels for Woodturning* by James T. Staley undercuts that claim, showing the ProPM edge lasts only 1.8 times longer. Even so, you still get better tool life for your dollar. The HSS gouge sells for $58.95. If you multiply that price by 1.8, you come up with $106.11. The price of the ProPM tool is $79.95 (2010 figures).

The table at right gives you factors you can use to decide whether powdered metal is a better deal than other steels.

Plain arithmetic is not the entire story, however. You have to balance the higher price of powdered metal tools with what you can afford and be realistic about your learning curve. Until you learn how to sharpen turning tools effectively, you are going to lose substantial amounts of steel to the learning process. This is especially true of bowl gouges. It is better to learn on inexpensive HSS than expensive powdered metal. Move to powdered metal tools when you have the sharpening skills to appreciate them and there is breathing space in the budget.

Powdered Metal Value Calculator

Start with the cost of a tool made from M2 HSS. Multiply the cost by the wear factor of the powdered metal version, from the table. If the result is more than the cost of the powdered-metal tool you want to buy, then the powdered metal version is a good value. Otherwise, buy the M2 tool.

POWDERED STEEL TYPE	WEAR FACTOR
M4	1.2
10V	1.25
ASP30	1.4
ProPM	1.8
T15	1.9
Rex86	2.0
15V	2.05
ASP60	2.4

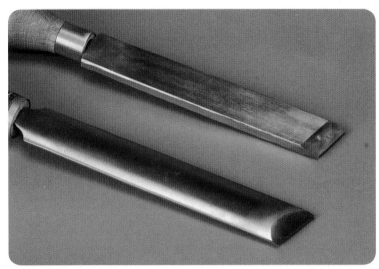

Traditional vs. oval. The oval skew (bottom) is easier for beginners to use than the traditional shape.

Skew Chisels

Cross-sectional views below show shape of blank from which each chisel is made.

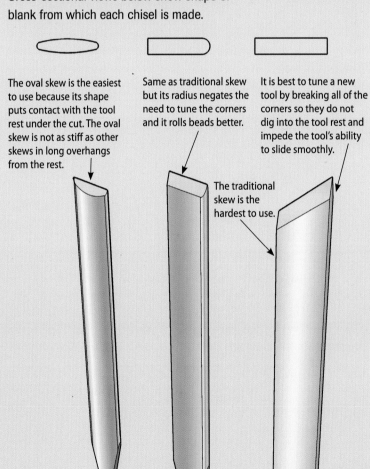

The oval skew is the easiest to use because its shape puts contact with the tool rest under the cut. The oval skew is not as stiff as other skews in long overhangs from the rest.

Same as traditional skew but its radius negates the need to tune the corners and it rolls beads better.

It is best to tune a new tool by breaking all of the corners so they do not dig into the tool rest and impede the tool's ability to slide smoothly.

The traditional skew is the hardest to use.

SKEW CHISEL

In early times, a woodturning chisel's edge was square to the tool's shank. Turners angled, or skewed, the entire chisel during use. Because the cutting forces constantly push toward the turner, he has to exert sufficient counter force to keep the chisel from skewing further and catching. Toolmakers quickly realized that by skewing the edge—that is, grinding it at an angle to the shank—they provided a more stable tool because the forces better aligned with how woodturners held the tool. Toolmakers also reaped a bonus because they needed less metal: A skewed 1" (25mm) cutting edge can be ground on a bar less than an inch wide.

The traditional skew is rectangular in cross-section. Most traditional skews have sharp corners on the rectangular blank from which they are made, which prevents them from sliding smoothly on the tool rest. One of the first steps in tuning a new skew is to radius those sharp corners with a grinder and buff the corners smooth. The corners of a rolled-edge skew are radiused at the factory. The oval skew is easier for beginners but lacks the stiffness of a traditional or rolled-edge tool.

The skew is one tool that must have a flat grind, because if it is hollow ground, it will catch in the wood much more readily.

The skew included in tool sets today is invariably too narrow—usually only ½" (13mm) wide. You will be much better served with a 1" (25mm) skew, because you can correct minor control issues before it is too late. With a narrow tool, the catch is over before you see it start.

Older 1" (25mm) carbon steel skews abound. Unless they have been burned in the grinder, they tend to be very serviceable.

Some skews are now made with a curved cutting edge, which is difficult to regrind and harder to hone while offering no advantage in use. Curved-edge skews are abysmal for cutting up to a shoulder.

BEADING AND PARTING TOOL AND THE BEDAN

Use the beading and parting tool and the bedan, two members of the chisel family, for sizing tenons. Either performs the task well, but the beading and parting tool also rolls beads and takes the place of a small skew.

My definite preference is for the beading and parting tool because it does more tasks, though both tools generally come from the factory with too short a bevel. I like the bedan ground with an angle of about 25°, and each face of the beading and parting tool, to 11° or 12°. The bedan can be hollow ground, but the beading and parting tool must be flat-ground if you want to use it to roll beads.

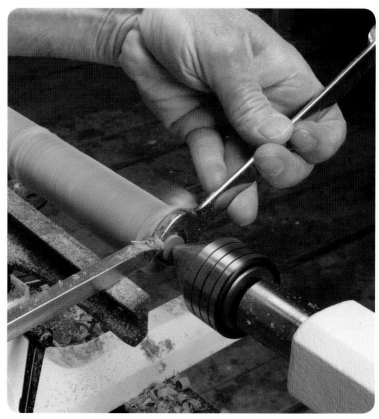

Cutting a tenon. A beading and parting tool in use. I am using an open-end wrench as a gauge, to tell me when the tenon is exactly the right diameter.

Sizing work. The beading and parting tool is great when used in conjunction with calipers to size the work.

Beading and Parting vs. Bedan

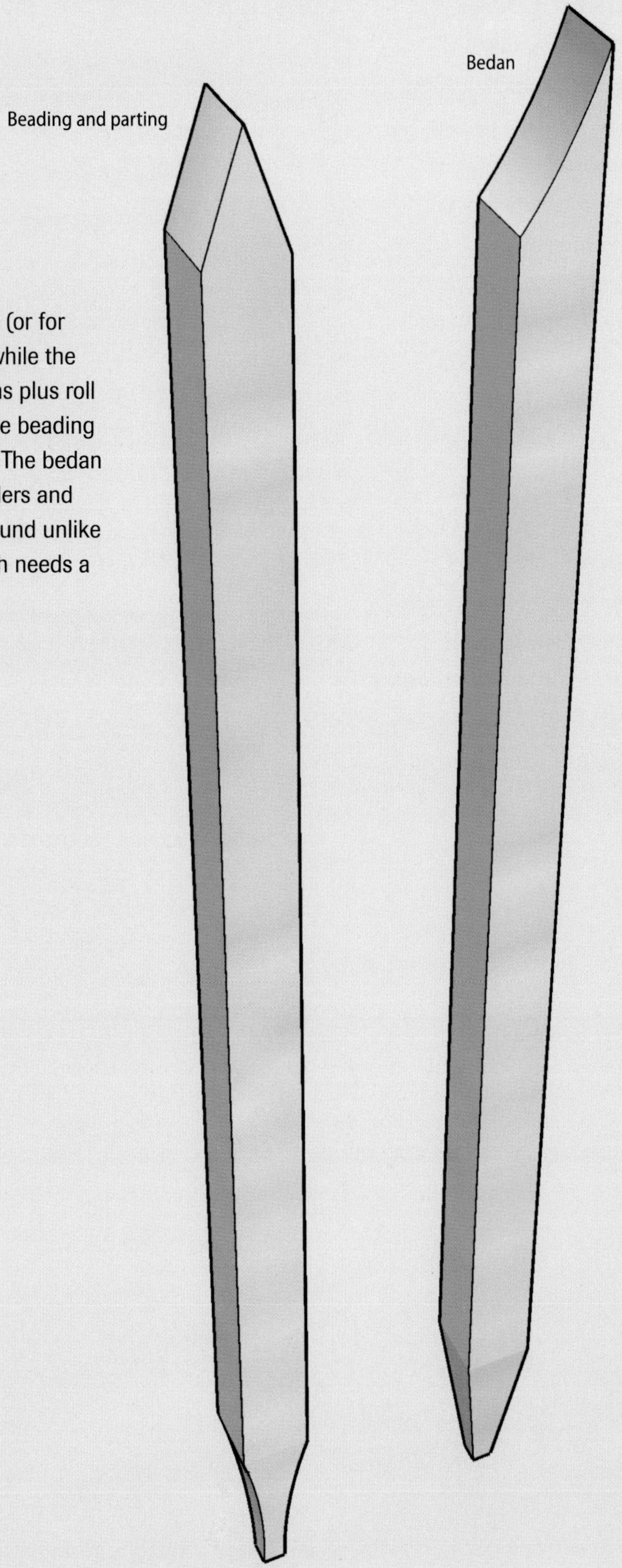

Bedan

Beading and parting

The bedan is only for sizing tenons (or for use with calipers for sizing work) while the beading and parting will size tenons plus roll beads. With its dual capabilities, the beading and parting tool is a better choice. The bedan is only used for cleaning up shoulders and sizing tenons so can be hollow ground unlike the beading and parting tool, which needs a flat grind like the skew.

PARTING, OR CUTOFF, TOOL

The parting, or cutoff, tool, another member of the chisel family, does just what its name implies—it cuts things apart on the lathe. It is also useful in conjunction with calipers to achieve specific diameters on spindles. A cheap parting tool is made from a rectangular section of steel, while a good one is diamond-shaped in cross section. A good parting tool produces much less friction in a spindle cutoff and provides more clearance in a faceplate cutoff. Parting tools are sold by the width of cut. I find the most useful size to be 1/16" (2mm), but it is difficult to find a diamond-shaped parting tool thinner than 1/8" (3mm) these days.

There are many newfangled parting tools on the market, all purporting nirvana, but in my experience they are no better than the traditional diamond-shaped tool. Most old carbon steel parting tools are diamond shaped and prove most serviceable. New or old, a parting tool needs to be sharpened infrequently and can be brought to an edge rapidly.

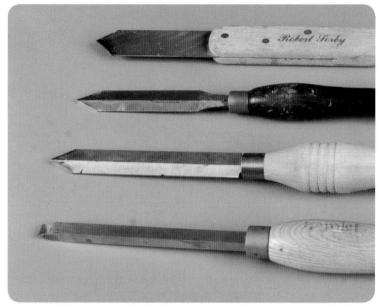

A quartet of cutoff tools. The extra-thin blade on the tool at top is useful when you want to separate parts of a turning without losing too much wood. The diamond-shaped parting tools and the beading and parting tool (bottom) are all-around workhorses.

Parting or Cutoff Tools

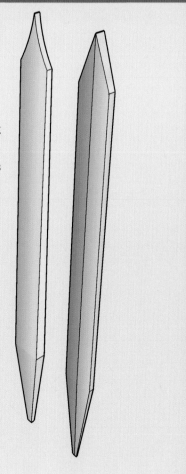

The diamond-shaped parting tool at right is far superior to the cheaper rectangular section tool at left because it has less friction in any cutoff. While the diamond used to be available as small as 1/16", finding them smaller than 3/16" wide is difficult today.

SPINDLE ROUGHING-OUT GOUGE

The spindle roughing-out gouge used to be called a roughing-out gouge. The American Association of Woodturners has endeavored to add the word *spindle* to the name to make it clear the tool is for spindle turning only. Faceplate work can break the handle, rip the piece off the faceplate, and scare the daylights out of you.

While a spindle roughing-out gouge quickly brings a square to round, it is also delightful for creating cylinders and fairing tapers. Sharpened to a long grind, the spindle roughing-out gouge rivals a skew chisel for cut and finish. While the skew is a wild animal that on a good day will turn and bite the best of trainers, the spindle roughing-out gouge is a loving pussycat that purrs even on a bad day.

Traditionally, the spindle roughing-out gouge was a forged, large, flat spindle gouge. Today, it is most often bent from a piece of flat stock or machined from a piece of tubing. The bigger the better, with ¾" (19mm) being the smallest useful size. I favor the traditional English style of grinding the face square to the axis of the tool.

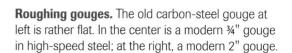

Roughing gouges. The old carbon-steel gouge at left is rather flat. In the center is a modern ¾" gouge in high-speed steel; at the right, a modern 2" gouge.

HOOK AND RING TOOLS

The hook tool is made by forging a hook on the end of a bar and sharpening the top edge. The hook tool was much used with spring pole lathes and made the turning of bowls between centers possible. In its original form, it is still used in Scandinavia but seldom seen elsewhere.

Commercial versions generally replace the hook with a ring because a tool-steel ring can be cast or turned inexpensively and the shaft screwed or welded to it. However, chips do not clear through the hole in the ring nearly as well as they do from a hook. Ring tools have partisans among box and hollow-form turners who find the tool good for end-grain hollowing. Although I have used ring tools, I have never found them any better than a spindle gouge for hollowing end grain. I think beginners should avoid ring tools.

Spindle Roughing Out Gouge

The roughing out gouge is now called the spindle roughing out gouge to denote that it is only for spindle work and can be dangerous to use for faceplate work. The tool comes from the factory ground to a very short bevel and should be ground to a very long one as pictured above. Buy as wide a tool as you can afford, up to about 2". Buying a tool larger than 1½" will not give better performance.

Hook and Ring Tools

Hook tools date back as far as turning itself and were part of the kit of spring pole lathe turners. The modern version of the hook tool is the ring tool, which lends itself better to modern manufacturing because it can be cast or turned. Ring tools are used by many for end grain hollowing where they work as well as, but no better than, a detail gouge. Small sizes of the ring tool work okay in dry wood but fail in wet wood because the center hole is too small to clear chips. Bigger examples are excellent for green wood bowls in a spring pole lathe. If used to turn green wood bowls with a power lathe, the speed should be kept very low. Normal speeds can be employed for end grain hollowing in dry wood.

Hook and ring tools traditionally were used with a rest much like a metal spinning rest. Pins act as fulcrum points to lever the tool sidewise in pleasing arcs. The tool is rotated considerably counterclockwise in use. Find a point where chatter is minimized and the cut is sweet. Very low speed—in the 350 rpm area—makes this tool sing.

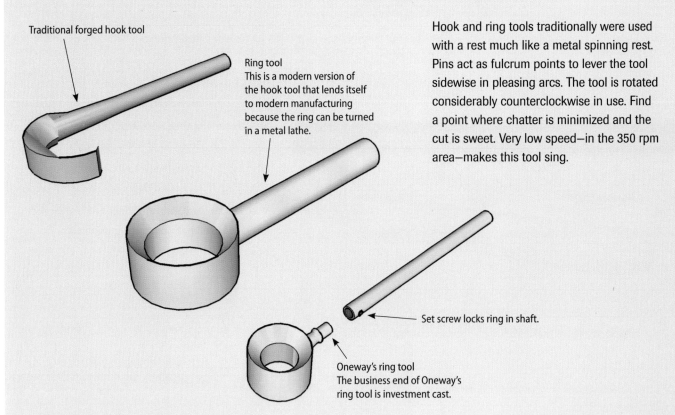

Traditional forged hook tool

Ring tool
This is a modern version of the hook tool that lends itself to modern manufacturing because the ring can be turned in a metal lathe.

Set screw locks ring in shaft.

Oneway's ring tool
The business end of Oneway's ring tool is investment cast.

Tools for Faceplate Turning

BOWL GOUGE

Unlike the spindle gouge, a bowl gouge has a deep parabolic-shaped flute. Use the bowl gouge with the shaft balanced level on the tool rest and the flute facing the direction you wish to cut. To cut to the left, for example, the flute would face about 11 o'clock. To cut to the right, it would face about 1 o'clock. The nose of the bowl gouge is ground to an angle of about 70°. The angle can be less for working on deeper bowls and greater for shallower work. Adjusting the grind that way helps keep the shaft of the tool from hitting the rim of the bowl and pushing the cutting edge away from the work. Grind the sides of the gouge, which do the lion's share of the cutting, to between 40° and 50°.

Many companies offer bowl gouges with the edge ground at the factory to the specifications of a famous turner—with a premium price to match. Famous-name grinds are not worth the extra money because you will have to re-grind the gouge to suit the needs of the work you are doing.

Three bowl-gouge grinds. The gouge at top left is an advanced grind that is good once you have gained some proficiency. At the lower left is a gouge with a grind that is a good starting point for beginners. It is best to stick with one of those two grinds. At the right is an incorrectly sharpened gouge. The nose has been ground too much, leaving the sides higher. It is almost impossible to start a cut with this grind because the nose cannot register against the wood.

Tools for Spindle and Faceplate Work

SCRAPERS

Scrapers are indispensable to the turner and accomplish many jobs that other turning tools cannot.

Most beginners think in terms of buying scrapers pre-shaped for a specific task, but many experienced turners wouldn't think of doing such a thing. Rather, they grind a scraper as needed from any available blank of metal—an excellent way to save money. It is possible to fabricate a scraper for the job at hand in just a few seconds and then re-engineer it for the next situation. Old files, screwdrivers, woodworking chisels, cement chisels, and even car springs make excellent scrapers. You grind them up and throw them away, so there is no reason to spend hard-earned cash on them.

Scrapers get a bad rap in some quarters. A few influential turners insist scraping is somehow inferior to cutting with a skew or gouge. As a result, beginners commonly believe there is something wrong with scraping. That is not the case at all.

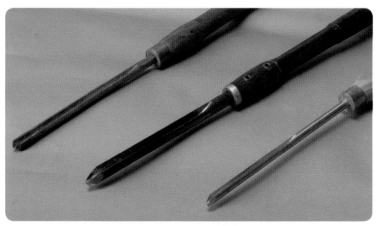

The ½" gouge at left is an antique, forged tool dating from the 1960s. The two tools to the right are modern high speed steel examples which are milled from round bar stock. While they look different they function identically. Center is a ½" Thompson Bowl Gouge while the one at the right is a ¼" Sorby.

It takes a lot of practice to be able to shape a perfect curve with a bowl gouge. The gouge cannot work on the inside of a bowl with a cavity deeper than the rim diameter. But a scraper can shape both the interior and exterior surfaces of vessels and remove material safely from spaces where no gouge can cut. If you think fairing a perfect curve is hard, it is even harder to make something like a platter perfectly flat with a bowl gouge. In addition, gouges and chisels do not inherently make things concentric. They cut a bit more or less aggressively in harder and softer parts of the wood and in face grain and end grain. But a scraper will machine wood to

A selection of shop made scrapers. Scrapers can be made from old files, chisels, and even a screwdriver. Shopmade scrapers can be ground to whatever shape you need, as this grouping shows. The bottom right is a commercial example re-ground to a boat tail shape for flattening platters and tabletops.

$ SAVING MONEY

Grinding Your Own Scrapers

A turning scraper is no more than a blank of metal that you can grind to the desired shape for the job at hand. The scraper is one of the easiest tools to sharpen. Set the grinder's tool rest for a 15° angle (the amount of steel to be removed, leaving the tool with a 75° angle on the edge), place the scraper flat on the rest, and touch the edge to the wheel. Immediately begin moving the edge to form the shape you want. For a straight edge, move the steel left to right. For a curved edge, rotate the tool against the wheel.

Grinding or burnishing causes the steel to deform and creates a burr on the edge. Burnishing produces the burr through direct force. Grinding produces the burr through a combination of forces—the force of pushing the scraper against the wheel, the lateral force of the spinning grinding wheel, and the heat generated in the process.

Grinding raises a burr that is sufficient for most work, but you can burnish a scraper by hand. Manual burnishing is easier if you are using an old carbon-steel scraper or one made from scrap, which are more malleable than high-speed steel. However, Veritas (*www.leevalley.com*) sells a tool designed to burnish even a HSS scraper. It is a simple fixture with a tungsten carbide cone. Once you have ground the scraper to the desired shape and smoothed the top corner with a whetstone, put the tool in the fixture and lever it against the carbide cone.

In practice, I use the Veritas fixture to burnish large high-speed and carbon-steel scrapers for bowl work and grind all of my small scrapers—especially one formed to create a specific shape.

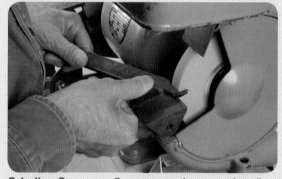

Grinding Scrapers. Scrapers can be ground easily from old files or any discarded metal. Here I am fabricating a special scraper to true the chucking recess of an air-dried bowl so I can grab it in a chuck and re-turn it.

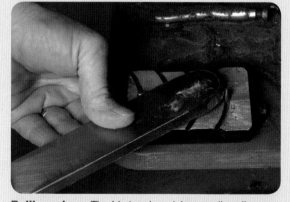

Rolling a burr. The Veritas burnisher easily rolls a burr on large scrapers with gentle curves. It is not as handy for burnishing small, odd-shaped scrapers.

$ SAVING MONEY

Making a Chatter Tool

The chatter tool is an interesting type of scraper. Made from thin steel and designed to vibrate, the chatter tool creates *chatter patterns* in end grain. It is a charming decoration for boxes and spindle-turned knobs.

Although you can buy chatter tools, they are easy to make from a piece of industrial hacksaw blade glued in a slot sawed in a handle. Scraping on center produces chatter marks radiating from the center, while moving the tool above or below center causes the pattern to whorl in opposite directions.

Chatter tool. A piece of saw blade, ground with a rounded end and glued into a slot in the end of a dowel, makes a good tool for embellishing your turnings.

Raising chatter. Hold the chatter tool like a scraper and let the flexible blade vibrate against the work.

Chatter marks. A chatter tool creates interesting patterns and textures. For details on how to turn this small box, see Chapter 5.

Making a Scraper from a Screwdriver

By converting a screwdriver into a right-angle scraper, you create a tool useful for removing wood from the inside of a hollow-form turning. (A hollow form is a spindle-turned vase-like vessel with a large interior and a narrow opening.) The scraper is the only tool that can reach into the corners to hollow the interior.

Screwdrivers are usually made of medium-carbon steel that has some temper, which is about right for a scraper. Heating the shaft allows bending to an acute angle without loss of strength.

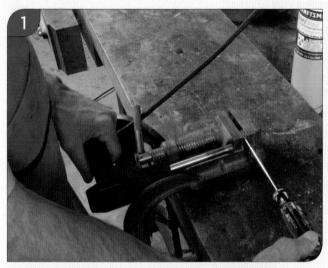

Clamp the screwdriver into a vise. Here, I have already ground the screwdriver tip to the shape I want. I am holding it in a drill-press vise I have clamped to the workbench.

Apply heat. Work from the two sides where you want the bend. This heats the steel faster and concentrates the heat at one spot, so the bend can have a smaller radius.

Begin the bend. When the steel turns cherry red, apply gentle pressure to the handle as you continue to heat the shaft. Stop when you reach the desired angle and quickly quench the screwdriver in water.

The finished scraper. Applying heat did not make the tip of the blade hot enough to draw its temper. The tool is ready to use and does not need to be re-hardened and tempered.

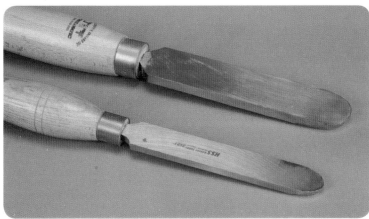

Dome scrapers. These round-end scrapers come in a range of sizes and are used for shaping the inside of bowls.

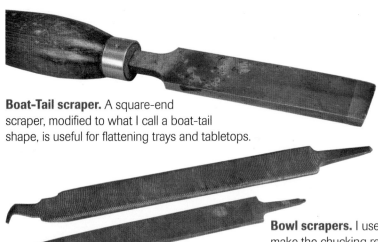

Boat-Tail scraper. A square-end scraper, modified to what I call a boat-tail shape, is useful for flattening trays and tabletops.

Bowl scrapers. I use scrapers made from old files to make the chucking recess of a bowl perfectly round again after it has dried oval. This allows me to re-chuck the bowl and turn it perfectly round.

perfect concentricity, making it the best tool for turning jam chucks, snap-fit box lids, and other pieces requiring a close fit. A scraper ground to the appropriate shape can repeatedly cut identical coves and beads.

The scraper leaves wispy thin shavings but does not remove much material at each pass. That is the scraper's strong suit. Because the length of the burr limits the cut, the scraper does not tear wood appreciably when working against the grain. That also makes a scraper very easy to control. Use the tool with a very light touch, always held like a captive bird. It can never fly away, but you never ruffle a feather. Because a scraper has to be held at a pronounced downward angle when shaping the interior of a bowl, I often hold the handle in my right hand like a pencil. This gives me a comfortable grip and a great feel for what is happening at the edge, hence, control over the cutting action.

A light touch. Always point a scraper nose down, so the burr on the cutting edge does its work. You can hold the tool almost like a pencil to sense how well it is cutting.

ARMREST

The armrest is an overlooked tool that you can think of as an auxiliary tool rest. It consists of a thick, rectangular steel bar with a right-angle hook on the tip that's attached to a long, sturdy handle. You balance the bar on the tool rest, support the handle under your forearm, and support the turning tool against the hook on the end of the bar.

In the eighteenth and nineteenth centuries, turners used an armrest so frequently that they hung it from a lanyard on their left shoulder for quick use. In those days, moving the tool rest was much fiddlier than it is today.

The armrest is most useful today with scrapers when fitting chucks. It lets you instantly adjust the height of the scraper's tip by simply moving your shoulder or forearm up or down.

Although you can buy ready-made armrests, you can have a blacksmith make one in a few minutes. Mine did the job for a six-pack of beer, but I supplied the piece of structural steel. (For an extensive listing of local blacksmith organizations, go to *www.anvilfire.com*.)

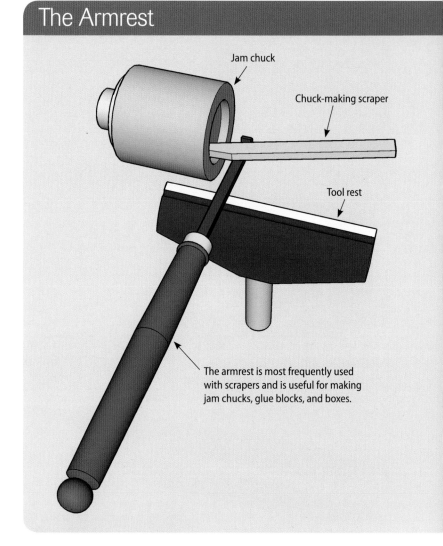

The Armrest

Jam chuck

Chuck-making scraper

Tool rest

The armrest is most frequently used with scrapers and is useful for making jam chucks, glue blocks, and boxes.

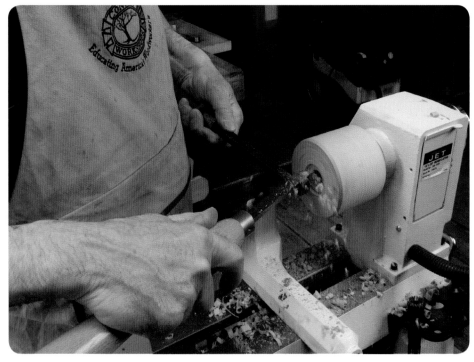

This tool functions as an auxiliary tool rest. Hold the armrest in one hand while using the hook at the end as a fulcrum to steady and support the cutting tool. As the photo shows, it is useful when hollowing boxes and chucks because it keeps support near the nose of the tool.

Measuring and Marking Tools

For measuring, I get by nicely with a 6' (1,829mm) folding wood ruler, available in any hardware store, and a 6" (152mm) combination square. A 12" (305mm) combination square works just as well. The square also has a center finder that allows me to quickly locate the center of any square or round workpiece. I often use the combination square to set dividers.

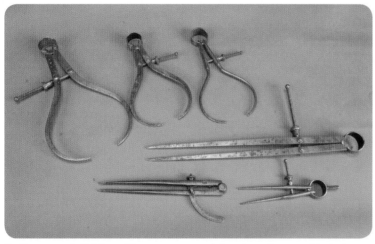

Calipers and dividers. These are essential tools: calipers, with their curved arms, measure the thickness of a turning; and dividers let you scribe a circle on the end of a workpiece, set the width spacing of coves and beads, or divide a circle into equal segments.

A pencil, a scribe, and several pairs of dividers do nicely for layout. For the scribe, I modify an awl by re-shaping the round tip square on whetstones. I do the same to the points of the dividers. I believe the square edge of a scribe makes as fine a line as a marking knife and will not cut screw threads when presented to spinning work, as a knife will.

I use dividers of all sizes for layout, allowing me to duplicate parts quickly. Using dividers to mark critical distances and the sizes of beads and coves is much more consistent than trying to transfer this information with a pencil from a ruler. Always make sure both legs of a pair of dividers are firmly on the tool rest and pointed downhill so that the points drag.

Trammel points can be thought of as big dividers. They are two metal points, like the end of an awl, that mount on a shopmade wood batten. Because trammels can scribe large circles, they are great for laying out bowls.

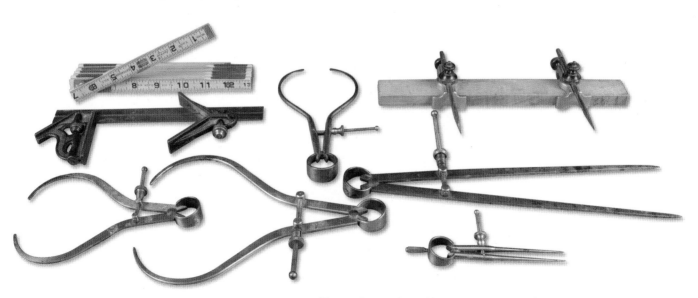

Measuring and marking tools. Calipers, dividers, rulers, and trammel points like those shown here are essential for accurate layout.

Making Your Own Tool Handles

When I was a young man, tools came both handled and unhandled. A frugal turner could save a bit of money by turning his own. I was one of those folks and took pleasure in making my own handles. Today, the only sources for unhandled tools are Craft Supplies USA, Packard Woodworks, and Thompson Tools. (See *Sources of Supply*, page 132, for contact information.) I still often remove the handle from a new tool and turn my own. Hand-turned handles can be graduated with the tool size, which makes finding a specific tool in a jumble much easier.

Although not necessary, a ferrule enhances the handle's appearance. You can use copper water pipe or brass tubing. Cut it to length with a hacksaw or pipe cutter. If you have sawn the ferrule to length, true the ends by fitting the metal over a tapered mandrel chuck (see Chapter 5, page 99) and cleaning up the ends with a scraper. Then press the ferrule in place. Shave down the handle if needed until you get a good press fit.

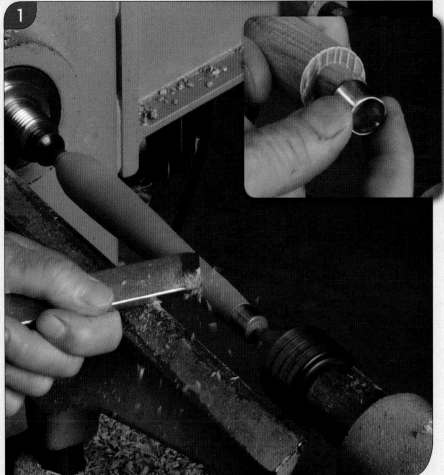

1

Shape the handle. You can use any good hardwood, such as maple, cherry, or ash. Begin with a billet about 1½" (38mm) square. Make it a pleasing shape that is comfortable in your hand. The tenon you make at the business end of the handle will depend much on the ferrule you decide to use. Around ½" (13mm), ¾" (19mm), and 1" (25mm) are all good diameters for small, medium, and large tools. If you plan to use a ferrule, turn a tenon about 1" (25mm) long (see inset photo), matching it to the inside diameter of the ferrule at the end where the tool will fit. Give the tenon a slight taper, which makes it easier to fit the ferrule. Turn the other end of the handle as close to the center as you can. Later, use sandpaper and a chisel to remove marks the center left behind.

Drill the handle. Drill a hole for the tool shank, using a drill chuck. If you are drilling for a tapered, rectangular tang (most are), measure the distance from corner to corner, about halfway up the wide side of the tang. Put the drill chuck in the headstock, centering the bit on the center mark in the billet. Catch the other end in a live center in the tailstock. Run the lathe at 200 to 300 rpm and advance the handle into the drill. Hold the wood steady with your left hand while turning the tailstock hand wheel with your right.

Finish the tool. Shellac is a great handle finish that can be applied in the lathe. With the lathe stopped, apply shellac with a rag or brush, then burnish with shavings with the lathe running. With the lathe still running, apply some carnauba wax and burnish the handle with shavings. Finally, fit the tang into the hole and rap the end of the handle sharply while supporting the end of the tool on a scrap block on the floor to seat the steel. Now you have a great, one-of- a-kind tool handle that cost next to nothing.

Finding Good Used Tools

In every class I teach, students bring in old sets of turning tools. I always get a bit nostalgic, as many are the kind I used when I learned to turn. Most of the old tools are carbon steel, but as long as you do not burn them in the grinder, they will work just fine—if they were good tools in the first place. The problem with old tools is sorting out the good ones from the bad ones.

A bit of brown rust that can be buffed off is okay, but if the tool is pitted, it may not be usable. Pitting will frustrate your efforts to grind a perfect edge, and the pits will get deeper as the corrosion worsens. If the tool has been burned in a grinder, it will need to be re-hardened and tempered anew. Look at the length of the tool and try to gauge how much steel has been sharpened away. A well-cared-for and little-used tool generally speaks for itself. Over the years, thousands of tools have been sold to people who used them once or gave up on turning in a few weeks.

Trammel points. Trammel points fit over a thin wood or metal bar and work like a large compass or set of dividers.

GOUGES

Spindle gouges can be hard to find. Many were made from flat stock, so they are too wide and have too large a flute, making them next to useless. The bowl gouge is even harder tool to find used. This is probably because the tool was not known much in this country until the 1950s. You will probably have to buy this tool new.

CHISELS

Most old skews and parting tools are perfectly serviceable. Older 1" (25mm) carbon steel skews abound. Unless they have been burned in the grinder, they tend to be very serviceable. They can be re-hardened and tempered.

SCRAPERS

Old scrapers are plentiful, and they work just as well today as yesterday. Their shape is unimportant because you grind scrapers to whatever shape you need at the moment. Never throw away any steel blank that can be made into a scraper.

MEASURING AND MARKING TOOLS

Calipers, dividers, and combination squares are among the easiest tools to find used. You can pick them up at almost any flea market for pennies of their original cost. That is because the toolboxes of thousands of machinists that populated the industrial towns across the United States are being sold off. Most were kept in great Gerstner wood toolboxes and are in great condition.

Used calipers and dividers were made by purveyors to the precision machine-tool trade by old stalwarts like Starrett, Brown and Sharps, Athol Tool, and Lufkin. These are precision tools that have a superior pedigree, with fine proportions and hardened steel tips. The tips of calipers meant for metalwork are often sharpened to an edge. A radius is better for woodturning and it is an easy matter to take the tip to a gentle radius with a grinder or coarse stone.

Tools You Can Live Without

Tool shows and turning catalogues are full of products claiming they will make you a proficient turner overnight. With the exception of the oval skew, which really is easy to use, I have yet to find a newfangled tool that lives up to its claims. Turning is a skill. It takes practice and knowing how to shape and sharpen tools properly. Those are the most important factors in gaining woodturning proficiency.

Every item in my review of useful tools represents time-honored designs that give superlative performance—in skilled hands—and the most bang for your buck.

CARBIDE CUTTERS

There are a number of tools coming on the market that use disposable carbide inserts actually designed for metalworking. While the cutters are the cat's pajamas for metal, they cannot handle the acute angles necessary for turning. They tend not to work well as scrapers either, because it is impossible to raise a consistent burr on carbide. The cost per insert change (the equivalent of sharpening) tends to run $5 to $7. That is far too rich for my blood.

I recommend avoiding carbide chisels and gouges. Carbide is a great material for cutters, such as router bits and saw teeth, but cannot withstand the long grind necessary for good turning tools. You need special, expensive equipment to sharpen a carbide cutting edge.

COMBINATION GOUGES

Combination gouges have a deeper radial flute than a spindle gouge but not the parabolic flute of a bowl gouge. The idea behind the combination gouge is it can be ground to a medium bevel and be used for both spindle and faceplate work. That is partly true. A combination gouge can be valuable for a bowl project's final clean up, but it is not a good spindle gouge. I prefer using the spindle and bowl gouges for their intended purpose and avoiding the combination gouges.

A Short Lesson in Heat Treating

If you buy used woodturning tools or want to make your own scrapers, you will need to heat-treat the metal to bring it to the proper hardness. You can do that with an inexpensive propane torch, although a costlier MAPP gas torch is better because it produces a hotter flame. (A propane torch costs about $25, while a MAPP torch runs about $55.) Max Power Propylene fuel—MAPP gas—is liquefied petroleum gas (LPG) mixed with methylacetylene-propadiene. If you want to make your own tools, I suggest using O1 steel, available from industrial hardware or mill suppliers. It comes in 18" (457mm) and 36" (914mm) lengths in a variety of rounds, squares, and rectangles.

Heat-treating steel involves three steps: softening (annealing), hardening, and tempering (heating to achieve the best compromise between hardness and toughness). Carbon steel turns specific colors at specific temperatures, and you use the colors as your guide to heat-treating.

Annealing softens the steel and makes quick work of fabrication. O1 steel comes fully annealed, so you can simply shape the tool and skip the annealing process when you heat-treat it. If you are re-hardening an old tool, begin by annealing it. Heat it to a bright cherry red color, and then plunge it into wood ashes, which insulates the steel and allows it to cool slowly. Then shape the edge and harden the steel. Again, heat it to cherry red, and then plunge it into a container of motor oil. (Used motor oil is fine.) If you are working with an old tool made from high-carbon steel, quench the metal in water.

Work in a well-ventilated area or outdoors, and wear safety glasses.

Although the quenching process seems rather casual, it is vital to ensure that steam pockets do not build up around the work and leave soft spots in the metal. Plunge the tool straight into the oil or water—nose down—and agitate it vigorously for 10 to 15 seconds.

After quenching, the steel will be as hard as it can get. A good test to see whether you have hardened the steel fully is to try to file the hardened edge. The file will skate rather than cut on hardened steel.

Fully hardened steel is so hard it lacks toughness. You have to temper the tool by removing some of the

Four degrees of tempering. Top left: The end of the bar is a pale straw-yellow, with a hardness of about RHC 62. Top right: This end of the bar is a deep straw-yellow color, roughly RHC 58. Bottom left: The end of the bar is bright blue, or spring temper, about RHC 50 to 55. Bottom right: The bar is light blue, indicating it has been heated above 640°F. The steel's temper is ruined.

Home heat-treating. To harden steel, heat the tip of the tool and as far back along the shank as the heat source will allow until the metal turns a bright cherry red.

hardness. Start by polishing the tool to a bright finish. Then slowly and evenly heat it with the torch, watching carefully as the metal changes color. (It is best to heat an inch or so behind the cutting edge and let the heat run to the edge so as not to overheat this area.) As a rule, edge tools such as knives and chisels are drawn to between pale straw-yellow to deep straw-yellow, which is between RHC 58 to 62.

One advantage to tempering by eye is that on a tool with a thin edge, such as a skew chisel, you can apply heat behind the edge and let the heat travel up to the edge. When the edge becomes pale straw-yellow to deep straw-yellow, the shank is generally bright or even light blue. That means the tool has hardness at the edge and toughness in the shank—a good combination.

Quenching the steel. Plunge the heated steel straight into a container of liquid. Use water if you are tempering carbon steel, oil for oil-hardening steels.

Heat-Treating Colors and Temperatures

(Hardness numbers are approximate and depend on the carbon content of the metal)

COLOR	DEGREES FAHRENHEIT	DEGREES CENTIGRADE	APPROXIMATE HARDNESS
Very pale yellow	430	221.1	RHC 61 to 62
Light yellow	440	226.7	
Pale straw-yellow	450	232.2	
Straw-yellow	460	237.8	
Deep straw-yellow	470	243.3	RHC 58 to 60
Dark yellow	480	248.9	
Yellow-brown	490	254.4	
Brown-yellow	500	260.0	
Spotted red-brown	510	265.6	
Brown-purple	520	271.1	
Light purple	530	276.7	
Full purple	540	282.2	RHC 54 to 56
Dark purple	550	287.8	
Full blue	560	293.3	RHC 48 to 52
Dark blue	570	298.9	
Light blue	640	337.8	

3 Be Smart About Sharpening

When I learned to turn, we sharpened our tools by feel, using a simple shopmade support mounted in front of the grinding wheel. It worked much like the tool rest on a lathe. Our ability to manipulate the tool against the grinding wheel demanded the same skills as turning itself. That is why I have always believed sharpening by feel is the evil twin of turning. If you have not fully learned to turn, you probably have not learned to sharpen. If you have not learned to sharpen, you will not be able to keep a good edge on your tools, so you will not be able to turn successfully.

Fortunately, you do not have to put up with that kind of catch-22. There is plenty of sharpening help available, in the form of a number of affordable and easy-to-use jigs. The ones covered in this chapter are those I have found most serviceable. They take feel out of the equation so you only need to concentrate on obtaining the correct profile every time you sharpen your tools. I cannot emphasize how important that is. The drawings and photographs in this chapter provide a good guide to the correct profiles for gouges, chisels, and scrapers. You should be able to duplicate the profiles with either a commercial jig or King Heiple's homemade jig.

Sharpening is key to turning. Without sharp tools, you will never learn to turn properly and most likely quit in frustration. Fortunately, there is a variety of jigs that help the process today, including this auxiliary table that is part of the Oneway Wolverine Sharpening System. It makes grinding scrapers child's play. I show plans for building your own system later in this chapter.

The Basics of Grinding and Honing

For any tool with a cutting edge, *sharp* means two flat surfaces meet perfectly. Using the tool wears down the cutting edge, transforming the sharp edge into a small radius. The tool no longer cuts well and needs to be resharpened—grinding one or both flat surfaces until they once again meet perfectly.

That is the challenge of sharpening. The heat of grinding and the force of the wheel cause the steel to deform, raising a burr that folds back over the edge when you use the tool. This leaves you with a small radius rather than a sharp edge. Ironically, feeling the edge with a thumb fools the neophyte into thinking the edge is sharp because the burr feels sharp. The freshly ground edge needs further work to remove the burr and bring the ground surfaces of the tool to the proper finish.

The abrasive quality of wood dulls turning tools. Some materials dull an edge faster than others. Teak, which contains large amounts of silica, dulls tools very rapidly. By contrast, clean hardwoods such as maple, cherry, and walnut dull much more slowly, so you can go longer between sharpenings.

The type of turning you do also affects how often you need to sharpen your tools. Spindle gouges need infrequent sharpening because they cut in a favorable way, across the grain direction in clean wood. A spindle gouge also cuts fewer feet per minute than a bowl gouge does. For example, a 2" (51mm) spindle turning at 1,800 rpm runs at just over 942 surface feet per minute (287m/min). But an 8" (203mm) bowl turning at 1,200 rpm covers 2,513 surface feet per minute (766m/min)—2½ times the cutting distance of the spindle gouge. The bowl gouge also cuts directly against end grain twice per revolution and bowl blanks often have bark that is full of dirt. All of that does nothing for tool life.

Tool Wear and Proper Grinding Angles

Spindle Gouge

At the very tip, a properly ground spindle gouge is between 25° and 30° with the angle increasing a bit along each side.

Chisels

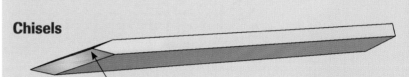

A skew chisel or a beading & parting tool is ground between 22° and 42°. If using the traditional rectangular, tool the beginner is well served to use the higher 42° angle and gradually decrease it as skill improves. Oval skews can be handled, even by a beginner, with a much longer grind and are often delivered at 22°.

Scrapers

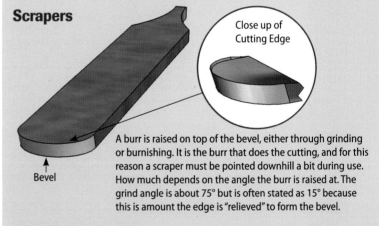

Close up of Cutting Edge

Bevel

A burr is raised on top of the bevel, either through grinding or burnishing. It is the burr that does the cutting, and for this reason a scraper must be pointed downhill a bit during use. How much depends on the angle the burr is raised at. The grind angle is about 75° but is often stated as 15° because this is amount the edge is "relieved" to form the bevel.

How an edge wears

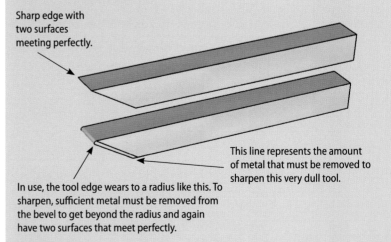

Sharp edge with two surfaces meeting perfectly.

In use, the tool edge wears to a radius like this. To sharpen, sufficient metal must be removed from the bevel to get beyond the radius and again have two surfaces that meet perfectly.

This line represents the amount of metal that must be removed to sharpen this very dull tool.

A typical grinder. It holds one coarse and one fine wheel. Important features include sturdy guards around the wheels and clear safety shields. Most turners replace the tool rests that come with the machine.

Choosing the Right Grinder and Wheels

People sharpen with power grinders, water-fed grinders, diamond plates, oilstones, waterstones, leather strops, and buffers. All of those products produce a great cutting edge, but some work better on one tool than others. There is no universal sharpening system. I have found the combination of power grinder, power buffer, and sharpening stones to be the fastest, most efficient way to sharpen turning tools.

You can also use a Tormek or Jet wet-grinding system. Both offer a jig that allows gouge grinding. Wet-grinding machines grind at a very slow speed, with a wheel constantly bathed in water, so it is impossible to burn a tool and take the temper out of the steel. I do not use wet sharpening in my classes because takes too long. It can take as much as 45 minutes to give a tool the correct geometry for the first time. That is too long for a gaggle of students. In a one-person shop, however, a wet grinder can be a useful but expensive machine.

GETTING A GOOD GRINDER

Grinders are available in 6" (152mm), 8" (203mm), and 10" (254mm) sizes, which refer to the diameter of the abrasive wheels they hold. The 10" (254mm) grinders tend to be too expensive for many people, and grinding wheels that size are expensive. Most dealers do not stock 10" wheels.

An 8" (203mm) grinder offers the best combination of speed, wheel size, and economy. You can buy a new one for as little as $80 or a reconditioned one for about half that. Most commercial sharpening jigs are made for 8" (203mm) grinders.

Some 6" (152mm) and 8" (203mm) grinders run at 1,725 rpm and are termed slow-speed grinders. Others can run at either 1,725 rpm or at 3,450 rpm. The slower speed gives you the best control over sharpening tools, so one speed is fine.

Do not worry much about the tool rests supplied with the grinder. Replace them with shopmade or commercial ones better suited for woodturning. Do choose a grinder with good guards around the wheels and sturdy, serviceable safety shields that allow you to see the progress of the grinding while protecting your eyes.

BEST CHOICES IN GRINDING WHEELS

Most grinders come with minimal wheels. The cheaper the grinder, the more likely the wheels will be duds. The first chance you have, upgrade the wheels. I have never gone wrong with Norton wheels.

Most manufacturers follow a set of voluntary standards for grinding wheels. The nomenclature used in the standards tells you what materials went into a wheel, how the abrasive is held together, how coarse it is, and more. The table below summarizes the terms. Understanding grinding-wheel jargon will help ensure you do not buy the wrong wheel for the job.

Consider the abrasive first. The wheels supplied with most grinders are typically made of silicon carbide. They will grind anything from steel to glass, but they grind especially hot. A much better wheel for tool sharpening is made of aluminum oxide. It cuts steel cleaner and generates less heat.

A second consideration in choosing a grinding wheel is friability, which is directly related to the amount of bonding agent used to hold the abrasive particles together. Abrasive cutting particles do get dull. As they wear, they become easier to dislodge from the wheel because a dull particle needs more force to cut; when the particle requires too much force to cut, it will break away. The trick is to find the right strength from the bonding agent so that when a particle begins to dull and breaks away, it reveals a sharp one. If everything works properly, you get a self-sharpening wheel. The right friability has a huge effect on the amount of heat generated during grinding. For tool-grinding wheels, a vitrified bond provides optimum friability.

A third factor is the size of the grinding particle. Most beginners opt for a fine wheel in the 100- to 180-grit range. That is a mistake. Fine wheels grind hot, but you want grinding to go quickly *and* coolly. To bring my turning students' tools to the correct profile, I use a 46-grit wheel. Once profiled, I use an 80-grit wheel for re-sharpening. Those sound like coarse grits, compared with sandpaper, but you cannot compare them. Grinding's high speed produces less penetration than hand sanding.

The final consideration is the space between abrasive particles. Just as open-coat sandpaper cuts cooler, so does a grinding wheel with more space between particles. The space gives grinding debris some place to sit until it can escape into the air. As the table below shows, the space between grinding particles is expressed as structure, on a scale from 2 to 16. A wheel with a structure designation of 5 or slightly higher is about right for small-shop use.

What the letters and numbers on a wheel tell you

PREFIX	ABRASIVE TYPE	GRIT SIZE	GRADE (FRIABILITY)	STRUCTURE	BOND TYPE
38	A, C, or Z	46 – 220	A – Z	2 – 16	V, B, R, E, M
Identifies the type of abrasive	A = Aluminum oxide, preferable for sharpening tools. C = Silicon carbide, an all-purpose abrasive. Z = zirconium, a good but expensive abrasive.	The best combination is a 46-grit and 80-grit wheel. Finer grits will only burn steel.	A to G = very soft. H to K = soft. K to O = medium, P to S = hard, T to Z = very hard. The best grades for a small shop are H to K.	Normal wheels range from 2 (dense) to 16 (open). A number 5 wheel is good for a small shop.	V = vitrified, best for tool grinding. B = resinoid, a bond for high-speed grinding. R = Rubber, a bond for high pressure grinding. E = Shellac, an elastic bond. M = Metal, a bond used on diamond wheels.

Sharpening Schemes

The platform rest is good for scrapers and the spindle roughing out gouge.

Use the gooseneck jig for grinding asymmetrical fingernail grinds on gouges.

This is an example of a shopbuilt toolrest that tuners in the past made themselves. Sharpening a tool without a jig uses the same movements as rolling a bead. Because, the bar mimicked a tool rest, it was good for sharpening by eye.

TESTING AND MAINTAINING A WHEEL

Before you attach a new wheel, test it for cracks. Hold the wheel in the air by putting your finger through the center hole. Tap the wheel with a metal object like a wrench and listen to the resonance of the tone. Just like a cracked baseball bat, a cracked wheel will produce a flat, dead tone. If the wheel doesn't have a clarion ring, exchange it for one that rings true.

Once you have attached the wheel, stand to one side of the grinder when running it up to speed for the first time. Then go have a cup of coffee and let the grinder run for five or ten minutes. Failures usually happen at, or just after, start up for the first time.

If the wheel survives that dynamic test, the next order of business is to refine its shape. A new grinding wheel is never perfectly round. Even a small eccentricity will cause the grinder to jump around and, worse, prevent good grinding because the tool will hop up and down uncontrollably. So install a grinding table (see the photo on page 64) and use a diamond dresser to bring the wheel perfectly round.

Whenever you use the grinder, always wear safety glasses and view the work through the grinder's safety shield.

Why a Skew Chisel Must Have a Flat Grind

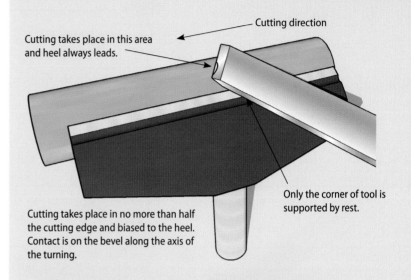

Cutting takes place in this area and heel always leads.

Cutting direction

Only the corner of tool is supported by rest.

Cutting takes place in no more than half the cutting edge and biased to the heel. Contact is on the bevel along the axis of the turning.

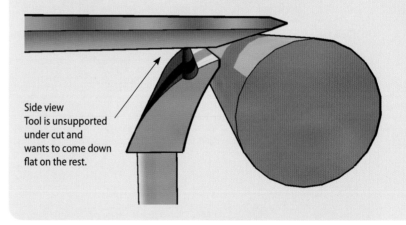

Side view
Tool is unsupported under cut and wants to come down flat on the rest.

Testing a new wheel. To check a new wheel for cracks, hold it by its center hole and tap it with a tool. If it rings clearly, it is okay. If the tool makes a dull thud, exchange the wheel for another.

Wheel dressers. These nasty-looking objects are designed to true and clean a grinding wheel.

Using Handy Grinding Jigs

A grinding jig guides your tool in a predictable way so you can get perfect and consistent geometry to your grinding. Jigs take one of four forms:

Platform. A small adjustable platform you can set a tool on is handy for grinding anything to a consistent angle. A platform is particularly good for grinding scrapers. Set the platform for the desired edge angle and you can then concentrate on the shape when you grind.

Simple shopmade bar rest. Before jigs got sophisticated, we often built a simple rest by putting a ¼" (6mm) bar in a piece of wood mounted next to the wheel. This essentially made a rest similar to a tool rest on the lathe. Sharpening with this rest uses the same motions as turning and we have much better options today.

Pocket jig. A long, adjustable arm extending from the base of the grinder, with a stop, or pocket, at the end to support the end of the tool handle. A pocket jig ensures you will give the tool a consistent bevel, much the way a grinding platform does. However, a pocket jig is better than a platform for grinding acute angles. It is a good jig for grinding roughing-out gouges, parting tools, and bedans. In combination with a gooseneck jig, it is ideal for grinding other types of gouges.

Gooseneck jig. Used in combination with a pocket jig, a gooseneck jig makes it relatively easy to grind the complex geometry of spindle and bowl gouges. The distance of the pocket from the grinder controls the angle of the grind at the tip, while the articulation of the gooseneck jig controls the angle on the sides of the tool. Changing one setting affects the other, so you have to play with the settings to find the right combination.

USING THE JIGS

For many years, the only pocket and gooseneck jigs available were the Oneway Wolverine System and the Oneway Vari-Grind Attachment. I could give exact prescriptions for setting these jigs that could be replicated anywhere. Today, there are quite a few jigs that work on the same principle as the Oneway products but require different settings.

You can also make your own sharpening system, based on one my friend King Heiple developed. Just follow the drawings on page 74.

To be certain you are using jigs to get the proper grind, use trial and error and try to match the bevel angles shown in the drawings on page 667. For gouges, first lightly grind the tool upside-down to produce a fingernail shape at the tip, as shown in the sidebars on pages 72 and 73, Then turn the gouge over, set the jigs, and grind until the fingernail shape becomes the cutting edge. Adjust the pocket and gooseneck jigs to settings that look right for the grind you want. Grind the tool and compare the result to the drawings. Adjust the jigs as necessary until everything looks right.

Sometimes you can obtain a correctly ground tool either by borrowing one from a friend or having him sharpen yours. You can now replicate the grind by blackening the bevel with a marking pen. With the grinder unplugged, adjust the pocket and gooseneck jigs until the edge appears to lie flat against the grinding wheel everywhere along the bevel. Now turn the grinding wheel by hand while lightly touching the tool to it. Check to see whether the black is scraped off everywhere. Change the jig settings as needed and blacken the bevel again. Once you can scrape the black off the entire bevel as you turn the grinder by hand, plug it back in and grind the tool for real.

Sharpening a Spindle Gouge

Define the fingernail shape. Place the tool upside down on the grinder rest and lightly grind the top of the tool at an oblique angle. The shape of the fingernail will reveal itself (see inset photo). The more oblique the angle, the longer the fingernail and vice versa.

Fit the gouge in the jig. Clamp the tool in the gooseneck jig with the correct protrusion. I use 1¾" (44mm). Adjust the pocket and the gooseneck to what looks right. A good starting place is with the pocket about 3⅝" (92mm) from the wheel face. Use a square or drop a plumb bob off the front edge of the wheel to measure this distance. Set the gooseneck angle to about 48°. Grind until the bevel meets the flat area that you ground in step one.

Tweak the jig settings. Adjust the gooseneck and pocket to correct any grind problems. Grind until you have formed an edge, and then buff it to a bright finish free of burrs.

Sharpening a Bowl Gouge

Define the fingernail shape. Place the tool upside down on a rest and very lightly grind the top at an angle of about 30°. The fingernail shape will reveal itself.

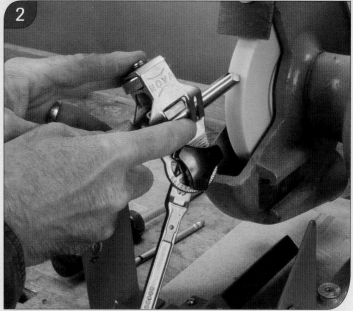

Fit the gouge to the jig. Adjust the gooseneck and the pocket to give a short bevel (about 70°) on the nose and a medium bevel (between 40° and 50°) on the flanks. A good starting place is with the pocket about 5⅝" (143mm) from the face of the wheel and the gooseneck at 50°. Grind until you have enough bevel to check symmetry. Correct as necessary.

Grind the edge. Once everything looks good, grind until you have formed an edge. You can go straight to the lathe, because buffing does not improve the performance of a bowl gouge.

$ SAVING MONEY

The Heiple Sharpening System

Spend ten dollars and a few hours to make this shop-built sharpening system,
designed by my friend King Heiple. It'll save you several hundred dollars.

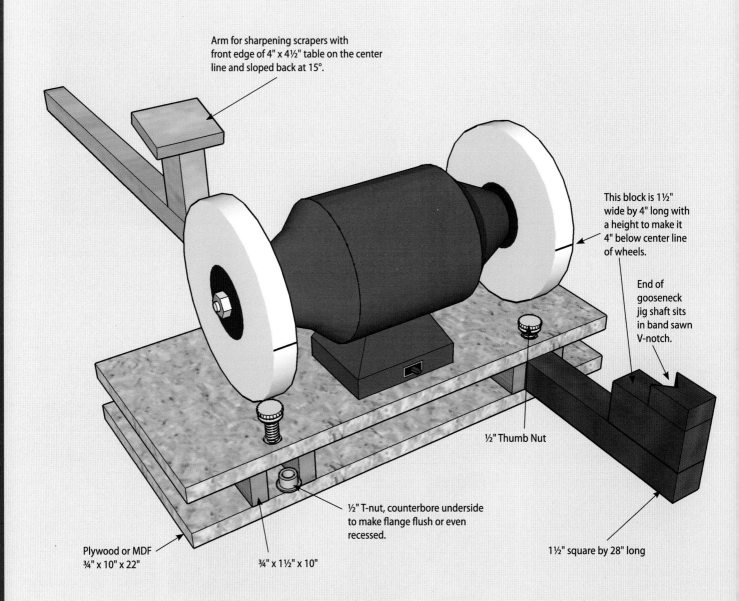

Arm for sharpening scrapers with
front edge of 4" x 4½" table on the center
line and sloped back at 15°.

This block is 1½"
wide by 4" long with
a height to make it
4" below center line
of wheels.

End of
gooseneck
jig shaft sits
in band sawn
V-notch.

½" Thumb Nut

½" T-nut, counterbore underside
to make flange flush or even
recessed.

Plywood or MDF
¾" x 10" x 22"

¾" x 1½" x 10"

1½" square by 28" long

King Heiple's Gooseneck Jig

Perfect fingernails every time.

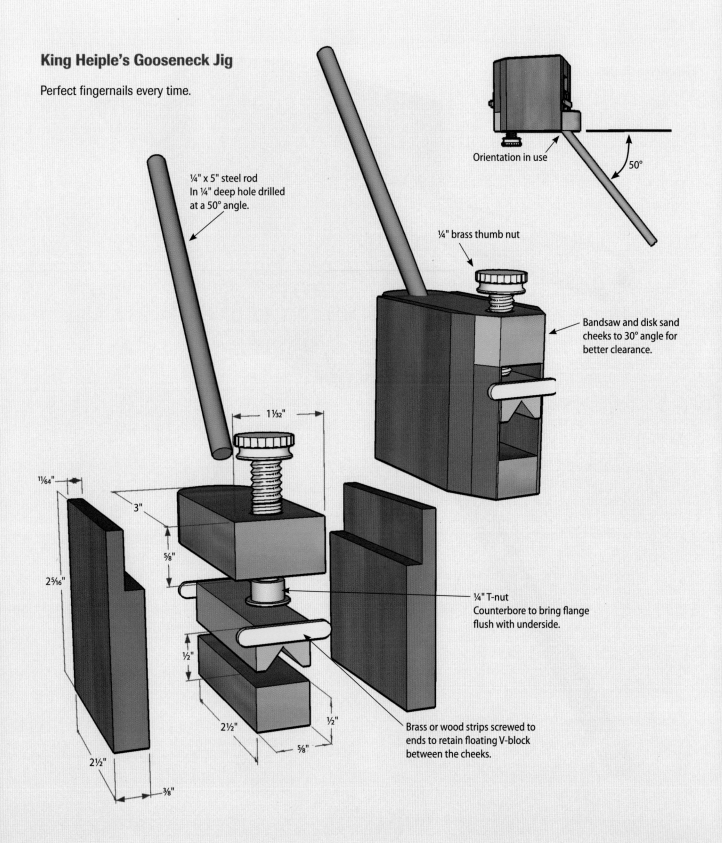

¼" x 5" steel rod
In ¼" deep hole drilled
at a 50° angle.

Orientation in use

50°

¼" brass thumb nut

Bandsaw and disk sand
cheeks to 30° angle for
better clearance.

1¹⁄₃₂"

11⁄64"

3"

2⁵⁄₁₆"

⅝"

¼" T-nut
Counterbore to bring flange
flush with underside.

½"

2½"

½"

⅝"

Brass or wood strips screwed to
ends to retain floating V-block
between the cheeks.

2½"

⅜"

$ | SAVING MONEY

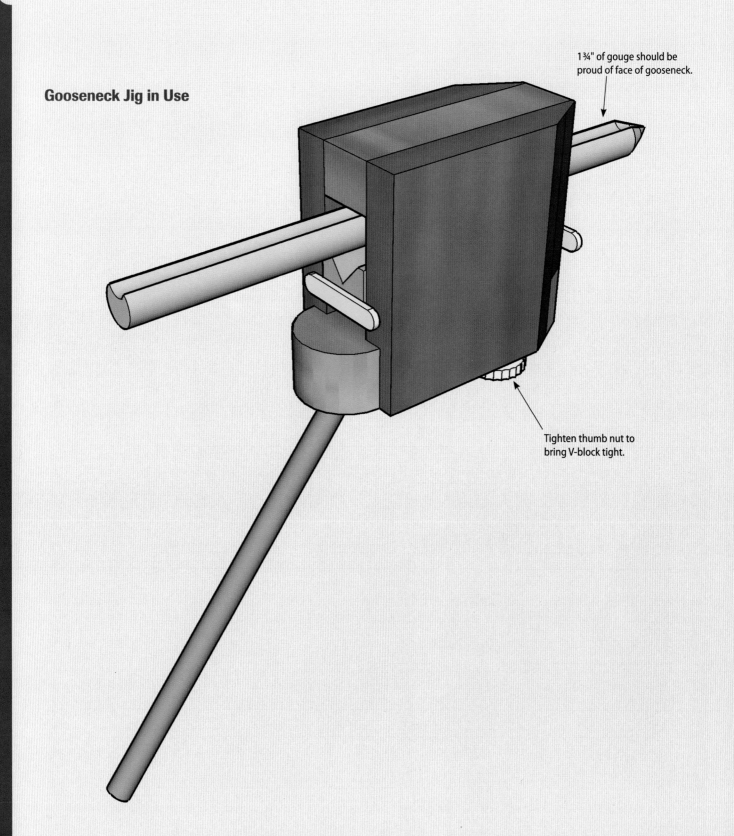

Gooseneck Jig in Use

1¾" of gouge should be proud of face of gooseneck.

Tighten thumb nut to bring V-block tight.

Honing: The Final Step to Sharp Tools

You can hone an edge by hand using slip stones, but a powered buffer does the job much faster. Use a dedicated buffer, rather than attaching a buffing wheel to the grinder. The grinder turns too fast for this work, and the buffing compounds will vaporize as fast as you crayon them on. I have found that a buffer turning at about 3,500 surface feet per minute (1,067 m/min) is about right.

The terms polishing and buffing are used interchangeably to describe this type of honing. Both use very fine abrasive compounds. But there is a difference. In polishing, the abrasive is glued to the cloth buffing wheel. In buffing, the abrasive is mixed into a wax or grease base, and you apply it to the wheel. The wax or grease base allows the abrasive particles to roll rather than dig into the steel, producing a finer cutting action that leaves the tool with a mirror polish.

You can purchase a buffer, but it is easy to make one from inexpensive surplus parts. I made mine from a motor I scrounged from a blower unit and a jackshaft I bought from a surplus store. It is not pretty but it works well.

If you do not want to buy a buffer or make your own, you can buy a buffing arbor from Beall Tool that fits in the lathe spindle. Or, you can buy an inexpensive buffing arbor, clamp it in a drill chuck, and power the buffer with the lathe.

THE LOWDOWN ON BUFFING WHEELS

Buffing wheels are usually made of muslin or felt. Muslin wheels, the more prevalent type, are either spiral sewn or cushion sewn, referring to the way the layers of cloth are held together. Cushion-sewn wheels are the more resilient type, giving them a milder polishing action. Both wheels are sold in ¼" (6mm) and ½" (13mm) sections. You mount multiple sections on the buffer to get the desired width.

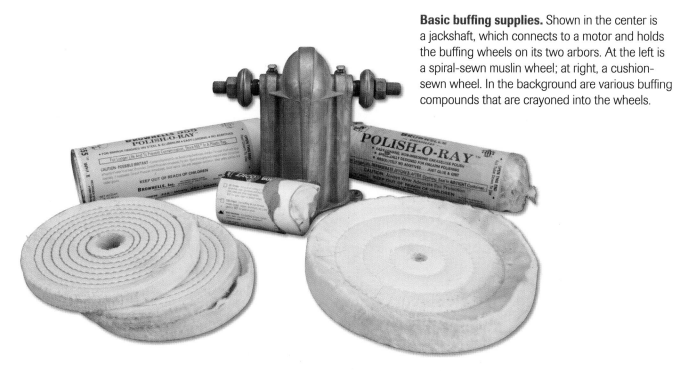

Basic buffing supplies. Shown in the center is a jackshaft, which connects to a motor and holds the buffing wheels on its two arbors. At the left is a spiral-sewn muslin wheel; at right, a cushion-sewn wheel. In the background are various buffing compounds that are crayoned into the wheels.

The right way to buff. It is important to hold the tool so the buffing wheel moves away from the edge, with the edge to be buffed held tangent to the wheel.

USING THE BUFFER

I mount a 10" (254mm) spiral-sewn buff on the left arbor and a 10" (254mm) cushion-sewn buff on the right. I apply what the finishing industry calls "greaseless" compound (sometimes termed satin finish polishing compound) to the left wheel. I buy it and all my other buffing supplies from McMaster-Carr. Greaseless compound is sold in several grits, like sandpaper. I use 180 grit for turning tools. The compound should be kept refrigerated until opened, and the open end of the tube should be kept in a close-fitting container with a damp rag in the bottom. If the compound dries out, the tube will be ruined, so you need to add water periodically. (You can usually cut the tube back a couple of inches if the end inadvertently dries out, saving most of the tube.) Crayon the compound onto the spinning wheel and allow 3 to 5 minutes drying time. On the right cushion sewn wheel, I crayon on a white wax-based abrasive called stainless steel compound (also known as chrome compound).

In grinding, the wheel moves *into* the edge. Polishing and buffing must be done with the wheel moving *away* from the edge. Place the tool against the wheel so the surface being buffed is tangent to the wheel, as shown in the photo above. If you don't align the bevel with the buffing wheel, you will round the edge and ruin it. I try to hold the tool at a tangent and contact the wheel just behind the edge. The wheel deforms at the contact point and bleeds to the edge. I use the left wheel to remove the burr produced in grinding and to polish away scratches that the grinding wheel leaves behind. Then I move to the right wheel to give the bevel and flute a mirror finish.

Whetstones and Slipstones

Turners have been honing tools with whetstones for hundreds, maybe thousands, of years. Whetstones can be divided into large, flat bench stones, for sharpening chisels and plane irons, and slipstones, for smaller handheld sharpeners. I often use them when I give demonstrations and it is inconvenient to take my buffer along. Even in the shop I use bench stones to hone my skew, beading and parting tools, bedan, and parting tools. A slipstone is an oil, water, ceramic, or diamond stone conveniently shaped to sharpen gouges. Bench stones and slip stones should be used with oil or water; it is just a matter of rubbing them on the bevel and flute a sufficient amount of time to remove the burr and to create a polish. It is good to have them in fine and polishing grades and work from one to the other just as you move from the polishing wheel to the buffing wheel with the buffer.

I use waterstones for honing my normal woodworking tools but prefer oilstones, ceramic, or diamond stones for my turning tools because they are hard and resist picking up divots from the pointed edges of skews and parting tools. Although you can use ceramic stones dry, I find soapy water makes them work better.

Using bench stones. Hand sharpening on oilstones or waterstones is the best way to put an edge on skews and beading and parting tools, which need flat bevels.

Finding Wood
4 Without Spending
Lots of Money

Wood is the one absolute necessity for turning that does not have to cost much. If you know where to look, you can find wood that is free for the hauling or available at a very modest cost.

Much of the free wood is green. While turning green wood is a pleasant experience, it can also lead to disappointment, especially for faceplate work. If you try to fashion a bowl from green wood without understanding how the wood changes shape as it dries, you will wind up with a cracked bowl. Note: Green wood will always dry oval but failure to understand why this is so can lead to failure through checking and cracking. Therefore, cracked or checked is the correct word here.

In this chapter, I will cover good sources for free or cheap wood, then give you a short course in wood movement to help ensure you will be able to turn free of disappointments.

Finding dried wood thick enough to turn a bowl is expensive, if you can find it at all. The solution that turners have been using since the birth of turning is to cut bowl blanks from a green log. A chainsaw greatly simplifies the process today.

CHAPTER

Finding Free or Cheap Wood

Overall, lumber is obtainable and inexpensive because most turning projects require minimal amounts of wood.

SEASONED WOOD

Most people who turn spindles prefer to work with seasoned wood. Finding wood is a matter of obtaining planks of sufficient width and thickness to yield the billets you desire. A spindle turner can often utilize narrow planks wood dealers have a hard time selling. They may readily offer a healthy discount. On the other hand, if you want wide figured planks, great for trays and small round tables, you may pay a premium for figure and width.

Cabinetmakers discard a good deal of wood because it is unsuitable for making furniture for one reason or another. The excess, known as drop, ends up in the dumpster and is often free for the asking. The skids and pallets under packing crates can also be a source of thick timber. Many pallets coming from the Orient will have mahogany-like wood in them. A resourceful woodturner can rescue this wood from the trash and turn it into useful objects.

You can even make good use of seasoned firewood for turning short, thick objects. Cutting back each end to remove any checking leaves a great billet. I often have students turn a carving mallet from a piece of red oak firewood.

GREEN WOOD

The turning of green wood is widely practiced by bowl turners. That is because seasoned wood quickly increases in price with the thickness of the wood itself. I can buy kiln-dried 1" (25mm) thick cherry for $5.20 a board foot ($5.20/.0024 cu.m.) but 2" (51mm) thick cherry is

New use for firewood. A stack of firewood often contains good turning stock. The handles and heads of these mallets were turned from wood destined for the fireplace.

$6.50 per board foot, a 25% increase in price for the extra thickness. If I want 4" (102mm) cherry, I have to drive to central Pennsylvania to find it— and pay $14 per board foot. The sharp increase in price reflects the difficulty in drying such thick sections and the extra time necessary in the kiln. Kiln-dried wood thicker than 4" (102mm) is almost impossible to find and extremely expensive when it does turn up. Green wood solves the thick wood problem handily.

Road crews, utility crews, and town maintenance people cut down trees every day and haul them to the dump. Generally, they will readily give you a section of log for the asking. Private tree-trimming companies may also give you some of the wood they cut.

With a little work, you can obtain large bowl blanks from those logs. Chain-saw planks 4" to 10" thick (102mm to 254mm) from either side of the center of a log, then band saw rounds out of the resulting planks.

Billets and Blanks

In faceplate turning the grain runs across the axis of the lathe, while in spindle turning the grain runs between the centers. It is possible to have work between centers and be faceplate turning and to spindle turn on a faceplate. It is the orientation of the grain and not how we hold the work that dictates which type of turning we are doing. Bowls are commonly faceplate turned while most furniture parts are spindle turned.

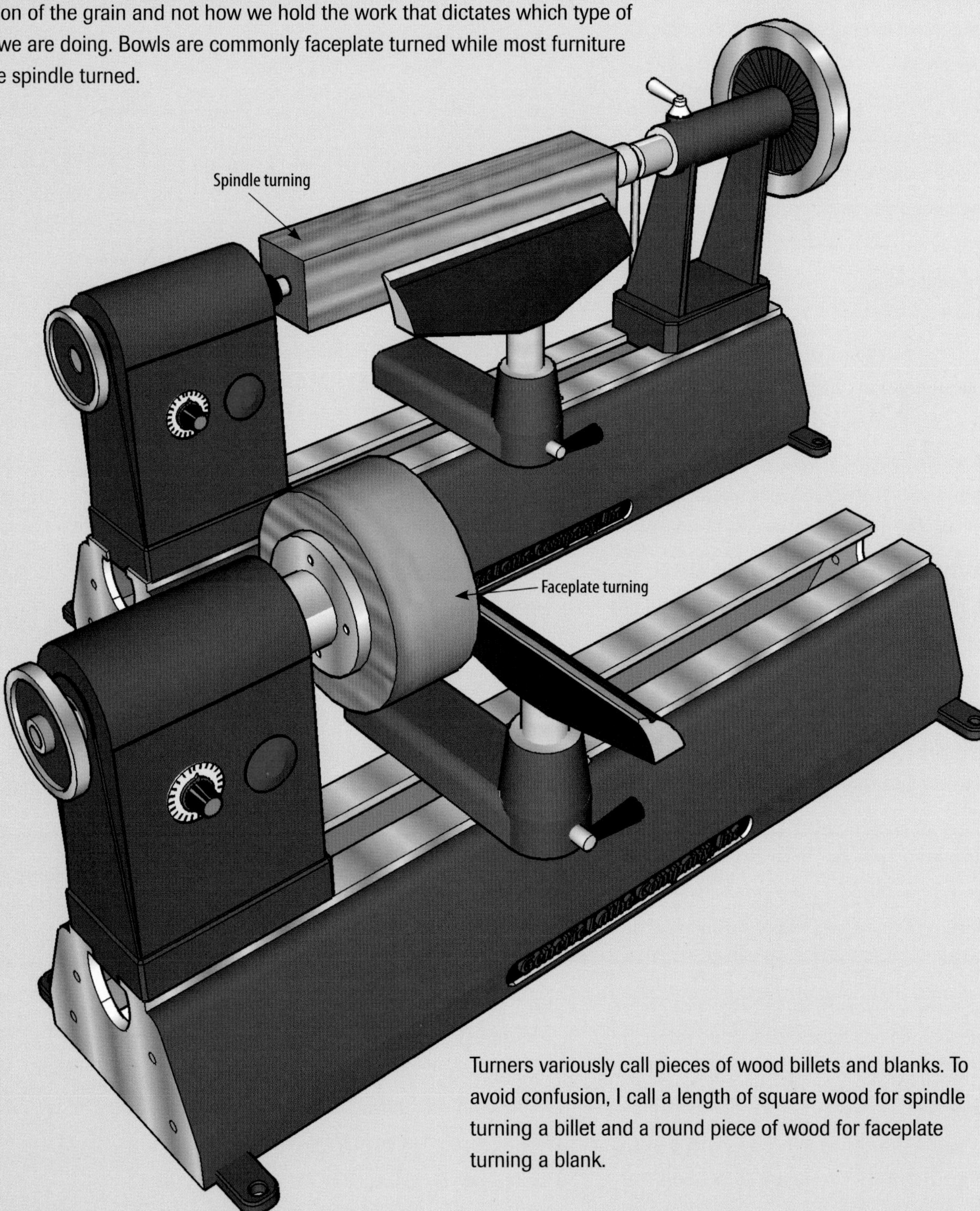

Spindle turning

Faceplate turning

Turners variously call pieces of wood billets and blanks. To avoid confusion, I call a length of square wood for spindle turning a billet and a round piece of wood for faceplate turning a blank.

Understanding Wood Movement

By understanding a bit about wood, it is possible to avoid many of the pitfalls that bedevil beginning woodturners and turn green wood with assurance.

Wood differs from metal or plastic because it does not expand and contract uniformly in response to changes in its environment. Instead, wood expands and contracts most significantly across the grain, with negligible changes along the length of the grain.

A felled tree is at least 60% water. When cut into lumber, the tree begins losing water. Initially, only the water around the cells comprising the wood fibers evaporates. When the wood's moisture content reaches about 28%, known as fiber saturation, the cells themselves begin to lose water.

Wood shrinks in three directions in relation to the original tree it came from. The first, longitudinal shrinkage, is along the length of the original log. On average, longitudinal shrinkage is only 0.1%, which we can figure as zero for our purposes. Of much greater concern is shrinkage in two directions across the grain. Across-grain shrinkage, along a direction tangent to the circumference of the tree, averages 7.95%. Radial shrinkage, perpendicular to the tree's center, averages 4.39%. Think of tangential shrinkage as loss in circumference and radial shrinkage as loss in diameter.

If we simply allow a log to shrink, tangential shrinkage alone will cause the wood to form radial checks, or cracks from the center to the bark. However, if we cut chunks of wood from the tree so that no chunk contains a complete annular growth ring, we end up with wood that more readily dries without cracking. (The entire lumber industry is based on this simple fact. The sawyer's work is to cut trees into boards without a complete annular ring.) When wood is cut this

Board Feet: A Common Measure

Big-box home centers sell wood by the piece or the lineal foot. Hardwood dealers typically measure and price their wares according to a measure known as the board foot. (Some exotic tropical hardwoods sell by the pound, and hardwood bowl blanks usually sell on a per-piece basis.) One board foot is the same as 144 cubic inches (0.0024 cubic m) of wood: A plank 1" (25mm) thick, 12" (305mm) wide, and 12" (305mm) long, for example, or a board 2" (51mm) thick, 6" (152mm) wide, and 12" (305mm) long.

Directly from the kiln, wood is rough sawn and sold in quarters of an inch of thickness (6mm). The minimum dryable thickness is 4/4 (pronounced four quarter). As there is allowance made for planing the rough sawn 4/4 board to a finished plank, rough sawn lumber typically measures between 1¹⁄₁₆" (27mm) and 1¼" (32mm) thick. This allows a cleaned up board in the ¹³⁄₁₆" (21mm) to ⅞" (22mm) range. Common rough sawn sizes are 4/4 (14mm), 6/4 (40mm), 8/4 (54mm), and 10/4 (67mm).

way, stresses that cause cracking cannot build in a circular pattern. The billet will not be square once it is dry, but it will have checking only 1" to 3" (25mm to 76mm) in from the ends.

Quarter-sawing—cutting along a radius (or close to a radius) of the original tree—provides the best boards. Quarter-sawing orients the wood grain to most minimize the forces created by shrinkage and by subsequent dimensional changes due to humidity.

In spindle turning, we work with squares of sufficient length along the grain to make the spindle we intend to turn. The orientation of the growth rings at the end of the square is unimportant, as long the billet does not contain a complete annular ring. If you are working with figured wood, the grain patterns are usually the strongest in the radial plane, where the wood has been quarter-sawn. If the billet is to be a table leg or stair newel, with square areas left intact, having the radial face show will add accent to your furniture.

Wood Technology and Bowl Blanks

Wood shrinks most around the circumference of a log and across its width, but little along its length. By understanding these properties, you can saw good turning blanks from free or inexpensive green wood.

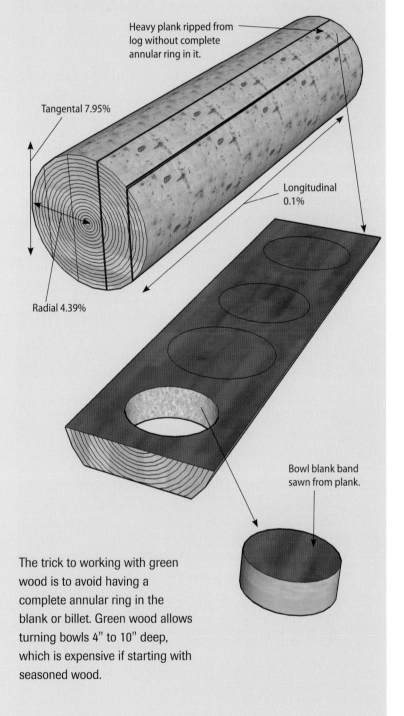

Heavy plank ripped from log without complete annular ring in it.

Tangental 7.95%

Longitudinal 0.1%

Radial 4.39%

Bowl blank band sawn from plank.

The trick to working with green wood is to avoid having a complete annular ring in the blank or billet. Green wood allows turning bowls 4" to 10" deep, which is expensive if starting with seasoned wood.

Spindles: Splitting and Riving, Then Turning

Early turners did not have the luxury of sawmills, table saws, or band saws, so they had to create their billets by splitting the wood from a clear, green log of suitable length—a process called riving. Modern turners can use the technique as well.

The turner first pounded wedges into the end of the log to split it into usable segments. He then reduced the size of the pieces by splitting them with a tool called a froe, which resembles a one-handled drawknife. The turner pounded the froe into the wood and then twisted to separate the pieces. Early turners knew the importance of riving equal masses of wood as the log grew smaller. If the turner removed unequal masses, the split would travel toward the lighter piece, further increasing the disproportion.

Splitting a log. Fashioning a turning billet begins with a wedge and sledge to split a log in half, then into quarters.

Using a froe. To split a piece further, pound a froe into the wood.

Fast split. Repeat the splitting until you have a billet of the desired size.

Finally, the turner used a drawknife to shape the wood into a roughly round billet. With riven stock, all grain fibers are parallel, which allows you to produce a much stronger finished turning. Despite having delicate legs and spindles, Windsor chairs are sturdy because they use riven stock. A fair number of modern Windsor chairmakers make their turnings from rivings they split themselves, in order to keep the dainty proportions of the originals.

Wood is much easier to turn green, and as long as the billet does not contain a complete annular ring, checking will not be a problem. Once the wood has dried, spindle turnings will be slightly oval due to the differences in tangential and radial shrinkage. However, you will not notice the ovalness of a spindle unless you run your fingers around it.

Finishing Up. A drawknife quickly makes the billet roughly round and ready for turning.

Green bowls. Turned from green wood, these bowls are deliberately left with thick walls so that they will dry without excessive distortion. In about three months, they will be turned to their final shape.

Turning Green Bowls

If you turn a bowl from green wood, it will change from round to oval as it dries. It will be perfectly functional, though. In fact, antique stores are full of oval bowls. That is how they were turned until the late-nineteenth century. Until then, people expected a wooden bowl to be oval.

Not any more. Call us the Tupperware Generation, but many turners, myself included, like a bowl to be round.

Creating a round bowl from green wood requires understanding of another factor of wood technology—the *elastic limit*.

Any material will bend only so far before it breaks. That breaking point is the elastic limit. With most materials, including wood, a thin section will bend farther and more readily without breaking. Therefore, a green bowl blank needs to be turned with a reasonably thin wall soon after you band saw the blank from the log. A thicker wall has a lower elastic limit and so it will not bend as readily as it dries. The wood is likely to check.

A good rule of thumb for wall thickness is to make it no more than 10% of the largest diameter. For an 8" (203mm) diameter bowl, make the wall ⅞" (22mm) or less.

If I turn a finished bowl from a green blank in one session, I generally make the wall between ⅜" (10mm) and ½" (13mm), which is well under the elastic limit of wood. The bowl shrinks to an oval as it dries.

To keep the bowl round, it has to be turned in two sessions. First, turn the green blank to the shape you desire but make the wall thickness 10% of the largest diameter, the upper edge of the elastic limit. Allow the blank to dry for at least three months. Then, when the wood has dried, re-turn the rough bowl to final shape, giving it a wall thickness of about ½" (13mm) or less. You now have a finished bowl that is round.

Green wood tends to lose water from end grain faster than from face grain. That is why most boards check on each end. There are two ways to ameliorate end-checking with bowls. If you turn the bowl in one session, sand and finish it while the wood is still wet. Oil finishes act as a vapor barrier to slow the loss of moisture from end grain. Even salad oil smeared on after sanding will accomplish this, although it will never dry hard. If you turn the bowl in two sessions, put the rough-turned blank in a paper grocery bag or wrap it in two or three sheets of newspaper. The paper creates a sufficient vapor barrier to slow the loss of moisture.

5 Holding Wood on the Lathe

Centers, faceplates, jam chucks, scroll chucks, vacuum chucks—anything that holds work on the lathe can be considered a chuck. Catalogs are full of them, and turners routinely plunk down more money for a single chuck (with a plethora of special jaws they may never use) than I did for my first lathe.

For example, a scroll chuck is quite useful for bowl turning. However, priced at $200 or more, it is also a big investment. I think it is better to improve your turning skills first by learning to use centers, faceplates, and improvised chucks. *Then* buy a scroll chuck if you still think you need one. At that point, your skill will have advanced to where the chuck will be useful. The chuck itself will not give you any skill at all.

Like transforming a discarded file into a scraper with just the profile you need, making your own chuck lets you tailor it to your work. With a commercial chuck, eventually you will have to compromise your work because of the chuck's limitations.

In this chapter, I will show you several inexpensive shop-built chucks that hold work solidly and efficiently. However, they are just a starting point, helping you come up with your own clever ideas for chucks.

First, though, a few words about the different types of ready-made chucks.

The number of surefire chucking solutions on the market abound. This is an area where a little work and ingenuity can save $20 to $35. A one time purchase of a Beall Tap for less than $30 allows for the making of hundreds of faceplates and other chucks.

Commercial Chucks

CENTERS

These are the most basic chucks. Centers are built on a Morse taper that is sized to fit your lathe. There are several types:

Drive center. On the headstock end, a drive center literally centers the work and provides the force necessary to revolve it against your turning tools. Traditional drive centers have a center point and two or four chisel-like tines designed to dig into the wood. The center point picks up a center punch mark easily and the tines transfer the rotary force. For turning odd-shaped billets between centers, a two-tine drive center holds the work better than a four-tine version. When turning a bowl from an odd-shaped blank such as a root burl, you can most easily begin shaping the work by grabbing it between centers. If you plan to turn only sawn billets with nice square ends, then it does not matter whether you use a two-tine or four-tine drive center. You can always grind away two tines if the need arises.

Steb center. I use a steb center for the lion's share of my spindle turning. It allows me to stop the work to inspect my progress without turning off the lathe. A steb center has a spring-loaded center point surrounded by a circle of saw-like teeth. Tightening the tailstock causes the teeth to engage and drive the work. To release the steb center, you simply loosen the tailstock about one turn while the lathe continues to run. The spring-loaded point pushes the work away from the teeth; the work stops spinning so it can be inspected. To resume turning, tighten the tailstock again. That is much faster than stopping and starting the lathe and repositioning the work between centers.

Drive centers. A two-tine and four-tine drive center, for spindle turning. The tines grab end grain in the work to hold it firmly. A two-tine center, though hard to find these days, is the better type for holding work with ends that are not square. You can make your own by grinding two tines off a four-tine center.

Steb centers. Three sizes of steb centers. The sawtooth end of the center is spring-loaded. Pressure from the tailstock holds it against the work. Loosening the tailstock slightly frees the steb center and stops the work from turning so you can check progress. They are my clear favorite for turning accurately sawn billets.

Tailstock centers. In the past, the tailstock held a dead center—that is, one whose end did not turn freely. The center was either a 60° point on a Morse taper or a cup (or ring) point. A cup point is a point with a raised knife-edge ring encircling it. The knife-edge prevents the center point from splitting the work. Turners greased either type so the wood turned on the center without burning.

Modern lathes come with a live tailstock center. It works much better because no lubrication is necessary and you can apply more tailstock pressure against the work. Live centers come in a variety of prices and configurations. Price dictates quality, but only up to a point. You have to buy a

Tailstock centers. A selection of live centers.

FACEPLATES

A faceplate is one of the most useful chucks you can own. You will never regret owning a half-dozen or so. All new lathes come with at least one faceplate. Purchased separately, though, faceplates from the lathe maker can be quite expensive. Shop around. You can find good-quality faceplates from other retailers as well as used ones.

Many beginners think they need a very large faceplate, 6" (152mm) or more in diameter. Not so. I cannot remember the last time I used a faceplate that big. For most full-sized lathes, 3" (76mm) is an ideal size. A 2" (51mm) faceplate is more practical for mini-lathes. Sometimes, the best way to turn a bowl is to glue the blank to a scrap block and screw a faceplate to the block. Doing so attaches the bowl's foot to the block. That way, you can turn the outside and inside of the bowl in the same session. But obviously, using a large faceplate will make it hard to turn a small foot on the bowl.

You do not have to buy all of the faceplates you need. With one or two on hand, you can easily make more of your own, using an inexpensive tap to thread a hole for the lathe spindle. The sidebar on page 92 shows what to do.

live center based on the type of turning you plan to do. Cup-point centers tend to be clunky and large, so it is impossible to turn spindles with a small diameter at the tailstock. The truth is, a cup center is useful only with split turnings, where two halves of the billet are joined on a paper joint. You can save a lot of money and get a better center if you go to an industrial-supply house and buy a 60° point live center designed for metalworking. It will be cheaper and contain higher-quality bearings.

Commercial faceplates. You cannot have too many of these, but they do not have to be large. 2" to 3" (51mm to 76mm) are ideal sizes.

$ SAVING MONEY

Making Your Own Faceplate

I have a 1938 Delta catalogue that offers a 1" (25mm) x 8 tpi tap for wood, fostering the idea that turners could economize by making their own wooden jam chucks and face plates.

The Beall Tool Company (*www.bealltool.com*) has revived this idea. Beall offers wood taps in all popular spindle sizes. Priced reasonably at $18 to $27 each, the taps allow you to make as many faceplates and jam chucks as you need. Believe me, you can never have enough faceplates.

Here is how to use the taps:

Lay out the blank. Use dividers and a compass to draw a 3" to 4" (76mm to 102mm) circle on a piece of hardwood about 1¼" to 2" (32mm to 51mm) thick. The spindle nose cannot protrude through the finished faceplate, so the thickness of the wood has to be greater than the length of the spindle. If necessary, glue two pieces of wood together to get sufficient thickness. You only need to plane flat the side of the blank that you affix to a faceplate. Good woods for making faceplates and chucks are beech, elm, maple, and sycamore. Band saw a round just proud of the layout circle.

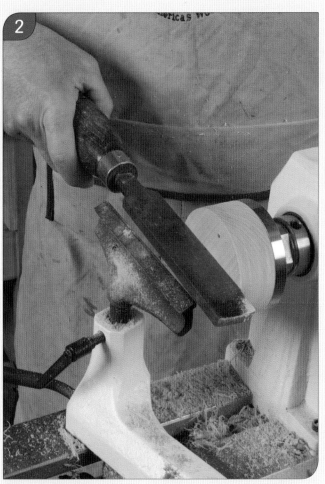

Attach a faceplate. Center a faceplate on the circle, drill pilot holes, and screw the faceplate to the blank. Mount the assembly on the lathe and scrape the face of the wood flat. The boat-tail scraper shown on page 55 is perfect for this. Check flatness with a straight edge. Now touch the toe of a skew to the center of the revolving work to produce a starting dimple for the point of your drill.

Drill a starter hole. Mount a drill bit that is ⅛" (3mm) smaller than the tap size in a drill chuck. For a 1" (25mm) x 8 tpi tap, for example, use a ⅞" (22mm) bit. Advance the drill slowly as it nears the end of the wood, so it does not hit the spindle nose when it breaks through.

Tap the threads. Fit a cone center in the tailstock. Lock the spindle, apply a liberal amount of mineral oil to the drill hole, and insert the tap. (If your lathe lacks a spindle lock, use a wrench or a tommy bar to immobilize the spindle.) If you plan to glue something directly to the faceplate, mineral oil on the glue face can prevent proper bonding. In such a case, use no oil at all or apply carefully in the bore only. Bring up the tailstock until the cone center fits into a dimple in the shank end of the tap, which will keep the tap centered. Turn the tap with a wrench.

Scrape a counterbore. If your spindle is not threaded all of the way to its shoulder, scrape a counterbore slightly longer than the shoulder. This will allow the faceplate to screw solidly against the spindle shoulder and maintain alignment.

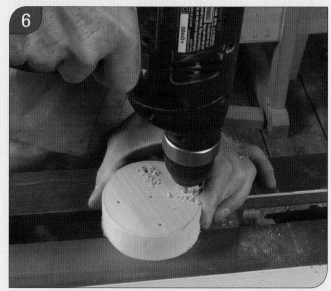

Drill for mounting screws. Drill clearance holes for the screws you will use to fasten work to your new faceplate. Use the same holes that held the wood faceplate to the metal one.

True the new faceplate. Mount the new faceplate on the lathe, making sure the side you tapped from is against the spindle shoulder. Use a scraper to make the blank round and chamfer the corners. If there is any runout on the face, scrape it flat with a boat tail scraper. You now have a useful faceplate.

FOUR-JAW SCROLL CHUCKS

The name stems from the scroll plate, which engages racks on the bottom of the jaws, causing them to open and close in unison when turned. There is a robust offering of excellent four-jaw scroll chucks. The least expensive are adjusted with levers. Small tommy bars fit into holes drilled in the scroll and the chuck body. The jaws open and close as the bars are pulled together or pushed apart. Better chucks are gear driven, with a geared key that engages a gear on the back of the scroll plate. Gear-driven chucks can be closed with much more force than a lever chuck. They are also easier to use, because you can hold the work with one hand while turning the key with the other. With a lever-driven chuck, you need both hands to work the levers.

A scroll chuck's jaws are two pieces. The bottom piece engages the scroll. The top piece attaches to the bottom with socket head screws. The two-part design allows one chuck body to accept an array of different jaws. These range from tower or spigot jaws, which close down on small dowels, to jaws that consist of large plates designed to hold rubber bumpers at various places to make a variation on a jam chuck. The photos on the facing page show some of the common types of jaws. Most chucks also accept a large, coarse-threaded screw that converts it into a screw chuck.

Attaching Work to a Faceplate

You do not need long screws to hold work on a faceplate. I usually use 1" (25mm) screws, which go about ½" (13mm) deep into the work. For very large work or difficult holds, I use 1½" (38mm) screws.

The best screws are #10 hex-head sheet metal screws. They have a constant diameter from just behind the point and a thread profile that gives them excellent holding power in end grain. Common wood screws and drywall screws make poor choices. A wood screw tapers, so it quickly loses holding power if a shock load causes it to withdraw even a small amount. Drywall screws are hard and brittle and can snap under shock loads.

If you are turning green wood, you can screw on the faceplate without first drilling pilot holes. When turning dry wood, drill pilot holes that are 70% of the screw's diameter for softer woods, and 90% for harder woods. The pilot holes significantly increase the holding power and prevent the wood from splitting. Use pilot holes for screws in end grain, which have only about 75% of the strength of face grain. Waxing the threads makes the screws drive easier.

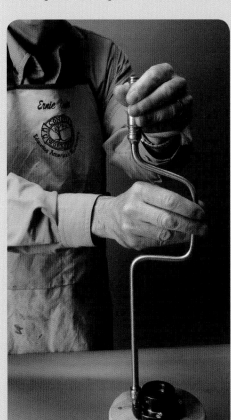

Better than an electric drill. While it is tempting to use an electric drill to drive the screws, doing so makes it easy to over-torque the screws, resulting in little or no holding power. I favor a mechanic's tool called a speeder, a long crank handle that holds a socket on the end. The speeder makes turning the screws easy but gives you enough feel to bring screws tight without stripping them.

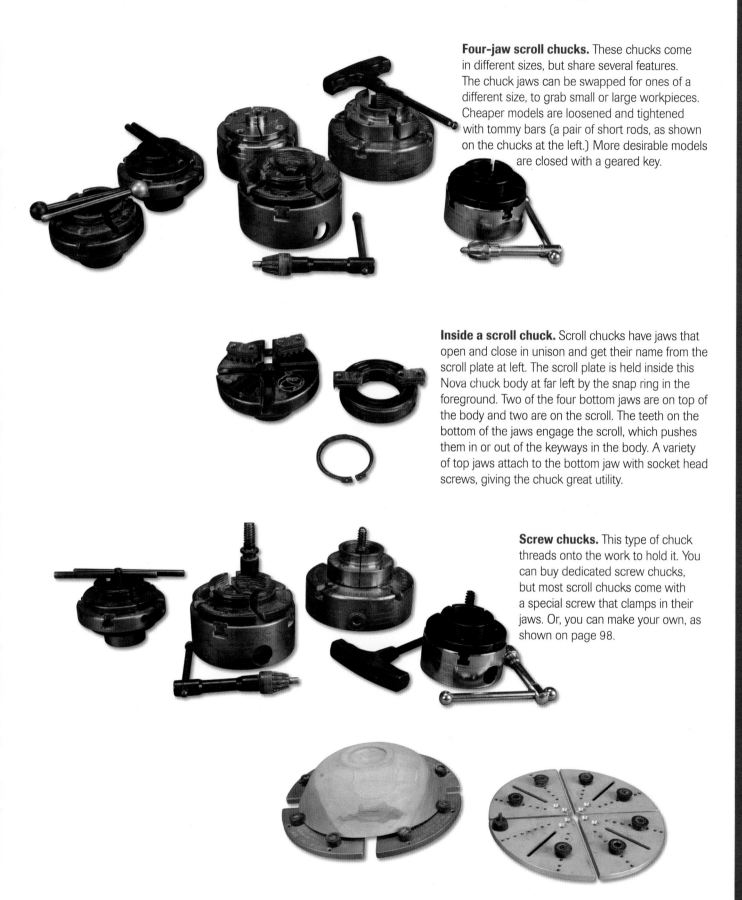

Four-jaw scroll chucks. These chucks come in different sizes, but share several features. The chuck jaws can be swapped for ones of a different size, to grab small or large workpieces. Cheaper models are loosened and tightened with tommy bars (a pair of short rods, as shown on the chucks at the left.) More desirable models are closed with a geared key.

Inside a scroll chuck. Scroll chucks have jaws that open and close in unison and get their name from the scroll plate at left. The scroll plate is held inside this Nova chuck body at far left by the snap ring in the foreground. Two of the four bottom jaws are on top of the body and two are on the scroll. The teeth on the bottom of the jaws engage the scroll, which pushes them in or out of the keyways in the body. A variety of top jaws attach to the bottom jaw with socket head screws, giving the chuck great utility.

Screw chucks. This type of chuck threads onto the work to hold it. You can buy dedicated screw chucks, but most scroll chucks come with a special screw that clamps in their jaws. Or, you can make your own, as shown on page 98.

Large chuck jaws. These extra-large jaws for a scroll chuck are meant to hold a bowl by the rim. But it is much easier to make your own jam chuck (see page 98) than to reset all those little rubber baby buggy bumpers.

Listed by the outside and inside range of diameters they hold, jaws have one place where they form a perfect circle. The jaws on an average chuck generally form a perfect circle at about a 2" (51mm) diameter. This size is best for bowl-turners. The chuck can either hold the outside or the inside of the bowl's base. For an outside hold, turn a tenon on the base and close the chuck jaws around it. Later, you will have to reverse the bowl, holding it at the rim, to remove marks on the tenon left by the chuck jaws. For inside holding, scrape a dovetail-shaped recess in the base of the bowl and expand the chuck's jaws in the recess. The closer you can make the tenon or recess to the diameter where the jaws form a perfect circle, the stronger the hold will be.

All chuck manufacturers have a system by which different inserts can be attached to the chuck body to adapt it to any common spindle size and thread. That means if you buy a different lathe you can adapt the chuck to the new spindle rather than buy a new chuck.

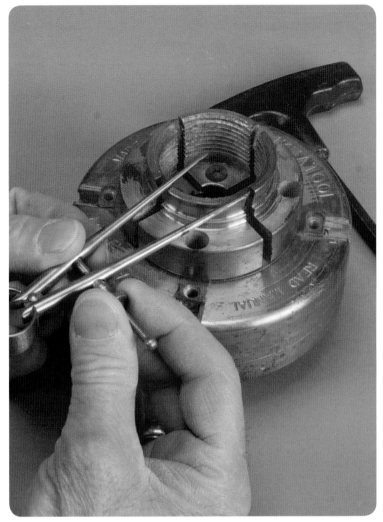

Finding the sweet spot. Scroll chucks hold best when the jaws are opened to the point at which they form a perfect circle. Here, I am using dividers to measure that point so I can transfer it to the work.

Dovetails. The jaws on a scroll chuck are tapered in a dovetail shape. Make a scraper with the same shape (see Chapter 2, page 52) to cut a matching recess in the work, so the jaws hold firmly.

DRILL (JACOBS) CHUCK

The lathe makes a great tool for drilling a hole. Think of it as a drill press lying on its side. Like a conventional drill press, the lathe uses a drill chuck, which has a Morse taper that fits either the headstock or tailstock.

To drill with the lathe, you typically chuck the work on the headstock and mount the drill in the tailstock. To center the hole on the work, make a starting dimple with the point of a skew. Bring the tailstock against the work, with the point of the drill bit in the dimple. As the work spins, advance the tailstock to drill the hole. With this method, known as gun drilling, the drill stays centered, avoiding grain irregularities, and yields a hole concentric with the outside of the turning.

You can also mount the drill chuck in the headstock and use the tailstock to push the work into the spinning drill. This is a great way to drill a short blind hole in long spindles.

In addition to holding drills, a drill chuck is handy for holding short lengths of wood for miniature turning—earrings and small knobs, for example. For this reason, it is better to get a ½" (13mm) rather than ⅜" (10mm) chuck.

Arthur Irving Jacobs, who founded the Jacobs Company in 1902, invented the first self-centering key-operated drill chuck. The generic

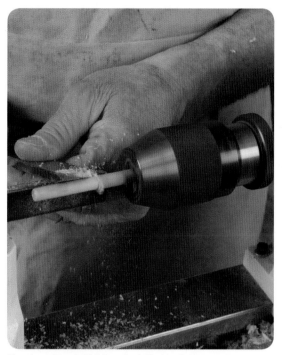

Not just for drill bits. A drill chuck is a great holder for small, short pieces, such as dowels or drawer knobs.

name for this tool is a drill chuck, although it is often referred to as a Jacobs chuck. But by rights, that name applies only to chucks made by the Jacobs Company (now a division of the Danaher Company). In 1932, the Josef Albrecht Bohrfutterfabrik GmbH & Co., located in Wernau, Germany, developed the classic keyless drill chuck. Albrecht's design has become known as the most consistently accurate drill chuck and is widely copied. Because you can hand-tighten it securely, a keyless chuck is safer than a keyed one around a lathe or drill press. If you inadvertently leave the key in a keyed chuck, it can become ballistic when you start the machine. That is why I would choose a keyless design over any others. Today, keyless chucks are widely made in the Orient for amazingly low prices—like $35 for a ½" (13mm) model. By contrast, in the late-1970s, my father and I each bought a genuine ⅜" (10mm) Albrecht chuck at a local machine supply house closeout. We thought we got a bargain, paying only $175 each.

Drill chucks. Left, an original Jacobs keyed chuck. Top right, a modern copy. Bottom right, an original Albrecht keyless chuck. On all, the Morse taper can be detached and changed if necessary.

Making Your Own Chucks

Turners have been improvising chucks since time immemorial, and they continue to come up with brilliant new ideas daily. Chucking is a way of thinking. The chucks shown on the next pages are all proven designs. Not only will they work for you, they will also help your brain begin to think in a *chucking way*. You will soon be designing chucks on your own.

First, though, a caution about speed. You do not need to turn at high speeds. If you are unsure about the holding power of a given chuck, keep the lathe speed moderate. You will still get the job done safely—and that is always the overriding concern.

SCREW CHUCK

This great chuck is easy to make. Mount a scrap of wood on a small faceplate and turn it to the same diameter as the faceplate. Then turn it cone-shaped, bringing the free end down to the base diameter of the thing you are making. Next, drill a pilot hole for a screw. The type of screw depends on the turning. For drawer knobs, use the same screw you plan to use on the drawer itself—otherwise, you can use a #10 sheet-metal screw. To make a heavy-duty screw chuck for holding bowls, use a ⅜" (10mm) diameter lag screw. Drive the screw through the faceplate and the wood so that enough thread protrudes to hold the work securely. For a knob, for example, the threads should protrude from the chuck as far as they would on the drawer front. You thread the workpiece onto the screw.

A Shopbuilt Screw Chuck

A screw chuck is a great way to turn multiple items such as chess pieces and drawer pulls and is a very easy chuck to make. Attach a scrap of wood to a face plate, mount it in on the lathe spindle and drill a tap hole on center with the tailstock. From the back, turn in a screw of the proper length to protrude ½" to ¾" from the block. Some cyanoacrylate adhesive on the screw before installation makes it stay put.

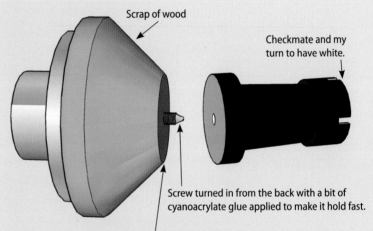

Scrap of wood

Checkmate and my turn to have white.

Screw turned in from the back with a bit of cyanoacrylate glue applied to make it hold fast.

The chuck may be turned to diameter of base of work. This eliminates the need for calipers in sizing the base. In this regard, our homemade chuck is better than a store bought version.

JAM CHUCK

Any turning book written before 1910 had at least one chapter devoted to making jam chucks. This is one of the handiest chucks in existence because it solves a host of problems. Unlike the jaws on commercial scroll chucks, jam chucks leave no marks. If you want to make boxes (small, cylindrical containers with friction-fit lids), you will need to use a jam chuck. A jam chuck also allows you to turn a perfect ball, which you cannot do with a commercial chuck. However, the biggest advantage of a jam chuck is that you can make it whatever size you need. Commercial scroll chucks dictate the diameter of your project because the jaws move within a fixed range. Because you control the size of a jam chuck, your design becomes paramount.

Jam Chucks

Although jam chucks are best spindle-turned, they can be faceplate-turned. I even make them for bowls from veneer core plywood and medium density fiberboard. The trick is to scrape a 3° taper to the recess so that it acts the same as a Morse taper, grabbing the work. Drill a ½" hole through the center of the chuck to facilitate a knockout bar for work removal.

3" to 4" diameter billet screwed to a faceplate and turned round. Optimally, the grain runs between centers (spindle).

½" hole to facilitate a knockout bar for work removal.

Opening is about ¹⁄₆₄" larger than workpiece.

The wall has a 3° taper inward making the bottom smaller than the opening. This makes it a wood Morse taper, locking the work securely.

A generous chamfer makes the edge concentric with the axis of the work, making for a straight and true jam.

Firm woods are necessary to make a successful jam chuck, especially if you are going to internally thread it to your lathe spindle with the Beall wood tap. Here are some of the woods I have had good luck with, in approximate order of suitability: dogwood, American beech, hard or soft maple, white oak, sycamore, walnut, and birch. Cherry and poplar do not work well.

To illustrate how a jam chuck works, consider the one I use to reverse-chuck bowls to remove the evidence of chucking on the base. Make the jam chuck from a band sawn circle of solid wood, veneer-core plywood, or medium-density fiberboard (MDF). If you are using plywood or MDF, wear a respirator. Use a heavy screw chuck or a faceplate to mount the disk on the lathe.

With the point of a dovetail scraper, inscribe concentric rings on the face of the disk. Find the ring closest to the diameter of the bowl you are working on. Scrape a groove wide enough for the rim of the bowl. Stop frequently to check the size of the groove, to ensure you do not make it too large. Taper the outside wall inward at about 3°. Tap the bowl into the groove with the fleshy part of your palm. To remove the bowl from the chuck, give the outside edge of the chuck a glancing blow with a gouge handle. That will flex the chuck enough to free the bowl.

There are some secrets to successful jam chucking:

- The piece you are going to jam chuck must be carefully turned concentric, and the face to be chucked must be square to the axes of the turning. If the end is not square, it will never run true. A slight chamfer (as little as ¹⁄₃₂" [.8mm]) at the edge also helps.

- The opening of the chuck should be infinitesimally larger than the piece being chucked. About ¹⁄₆₄" (0.4mm) to ¹⁄₃₂" (0.8mm) is about right.

- The chuck needs to have the same internal taper as a Morse taper, about 3° inclusive, or 1½° on each side. With less taper, the work will tend to bottom out in the chuck and will not be held tight enough. With more taper, the chuck will not grab the workpiece at all. But if the taper is right and the bore size is spot on, you will be able to insert the work in the chuck by hand, but use a hammer to seat it firmly.

- You seldom use a skew around a jam chuck, so you only need to master the use of the gouge.

The first few times you use a jam chuck will be frustrating, but persevere. You will get the hang of it and gain skill quickly.

Making a Jam Chuck and Using It to Turn a Box

While it is child's play to screw a suitable block of wood to a faceplate, wood taps from the Beall Tool Company offer great economy because they allow you to tap threads directly into the wood itself to make a jam chuck. Spindle-turned jam chucks work best with the wood grain running the length of the chuck. While Beall cautions against tapping a hole drilled into end grain, I have consistently done it successfully. Liberal amounts of mineral oil during tapping, as well as consistent tailstock pressure against the tap, are necessary, and you need to use a favorable fine-grained wood.

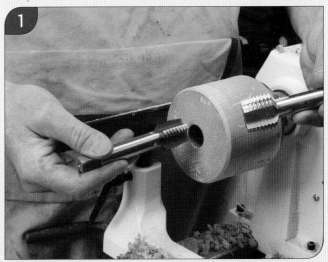

Shape the blank. Screw a faceplate to an end grain side of the block. Mount the work on the lathe, true it up with a gouge, scrape the face flat, and drill a tap hole ⅛" (3mm) smaller than the tap diameter. For safety, support the block with the tailstock while you true it up. Drill the tap hole about twice as deep as the length of your lathe's spindle.

Use the tap to thread the hole. Lock the lathe's headstock so the blank cannot move. Use a wrench or a tommy bar if your lathe does not have a spindle lock. Mount the Beall tap in the tailstock and move it up to the block. Drive the tap into the hole by turning the tap with a wrench, while you turn the tailstock's handwheel to keep constant pressure on the tap. Use plenty of mineral oil for lubrication. If your spindle is not threaded all of the way to its shoulder, scrape a counterbore slightly longer than the shoulder. This will allow the faceplate to screw home solid against the spindle shoulder and maintain alignment. Remove the work from the faceplate and thread the freshly tapped hole onto the spindle. Mount a drill chuck in the tailstock and drill a ½" (13mm) hole through to meet the hole you just tapped. This will allow you to slide a knockout bar through to knock work out of the chuck. Your jam chuck is nearly done. Remove it from the lathe.

Rough the blank for the box. Mount the wood for your box between centers and turn it to as straight a cylinder as you can manage. Use a spindle gouge or a roughing-out gouge for this. Square both ends and use a spindle gouge to put a small chamfer on each end. Remove this piece from the lathe.

Cut an opening in the jam chuck. Mount the jam chuck and scrape an opening in the end that is a hair larger than the cylinder you just turned for the box. It is important to taper the sides of the opening slightly, like a Morse taper.

Jam the work into the chuck. With the lathe stopped, use a small mallet to tap the cylinder into the chuck. Use the headstock handwheel to turn the work and check for runout, or wobble. Look at the far edge of the work as you turn it slowly. When it appears the farthest away, tap on the opposite side as shown in the photo to move it back to center. Keep turning and tapping until there is no perceptible runout.

Shape the outside of the box. Use a spindle gouge to shape the outside of the box. Use the same gouge to trim away the dimple from the centerpoint on what will be the base of the box. Remove enough material to get below any tearout, and undercut the base slightly so the box will sit level.

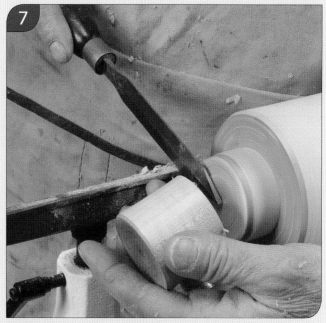

Separate the base and the lid. Use a thin parting tool to separate the base from the top. Set the base aside.

Making a Jam Chuck and Using It to Turn a Box (continued)

Hollow out the top. Begin by using a spindle gouge to dish the center very slightly. This will ensure that the top fits onto the bottom with no gap. Continue removing wood with the spindle gouge. With the tip of the tool exactly on center and rotated clockwise 15° to 20°, push it into the wood and pull the gouge sideways. If the flute points to the 12 o'clock position, the tool will catch in the wood.

Scrape a straight wall. Scrape a straight wall on the lid. Be sure the wall is straight and does not taper. Think of this as a mortise. You will turn the mating tenon on the base later. If you want to finish the inside of the top, do that now. Do not sand the mortise, though, or you will put it out of round and the lid will not fit well on the base. Use a knockout bar to remove the lid from the chuck.

Hollow the base. Remount the base in the chuck, correct any runout, and use a spindle gouge to remove the waste from the inside. When making a deep box, save time by drilling away most of the waste with a Forstner bit. I like to put a reverse taper on the inside walls of my boxes to match the outside taper, using scrapers I grind for the task. Sand and finish the inside of the base.

11

Scrape a tenon for the lid. Scrape a tenon on the rim of the base. I begin the tenon, put a healthy chamfer on the end, and then check the fit of the lid. If it will not slip over the chamfer, scrape down to the chamfer and cut a new chamfer. Once the lid fits over the chamfer, scrape the tenon very lightly and carefully, checking the fit often, until you get a nice friction fit. You can apply carnauba wax to the tenon to help the lid slip on. Twist the lid to align the grain with the base.

12

Shape the outside of the lid. Fit the lid onto the body of the box. The friction fit holds it in place while you turn the outside of the lid to match the body and give it a pleasing shape that complements the shape of the base. Then sand and finish the cap to your liking.

13

Add some texture and you are done. If you wish, you can add some texture. For example, you can use a chatter tool (see Chapter 2, page 53) to make a band on the lid, and set it off by incising grooves with the point of a skew or scraper.

A Typical Bowl-Turning Session

Setdivers. Use the chuck to size the base. Adjust the jaws to where they form a perfect circle and adjust a pair of dividers to the radius of the outside diameter the jaws form.

Screw the blank onto the chuck. Fit the scroll chuck's wood screw accessory into the jaws and tighten them. Drill a pilot hole into blank and thread it onto the screw.

Turn the outside of the bowl. Turn the outside and foot of the bowl, and scrape a recess about ⅛" (3.2mm) deep into the center of the foot. Use the dividers set in step 1 to mark the size of the recess in the foot, where the chuck will hold the blank. Taper the wall of the recess so it is larger at the bottom than the top, corresponding to the dovetail shape of the chuck jaws. The jaws will hold the bowl more securely.

Reverse the turning. Unscrew the bowl and remove the screw. Expand the chuck jaws inside the recess and make sure the bowl spins true with no runout. Turn the inside of the bowl. Sand the bowl and give it a coat of finish.

Clean up the foot. Remove the bowl and reattach the wood screw. Thread a circle of plywood or in this case a piece of scrap pine onto the screw and scrape a groove in it sized to the bowl rim. Jam-fit the bowl into the groove and turn the foot to remove chuck marks.

The finished bowl with no sign of chucking marks.

TAPERED MANDREL

If a jam chuck is yin, the tapered mandrel is yang. It is one of the best ways to chuck a billet drilled with either a blind or through hole—a pepper mill, for example. The blank for a pepper mill has stepped holes that are often drilled in a drill press before turning. The tapered mandrel is a slightly tapered shaft that fits into the holes in the blank. You turn the mandrel between centers, giving it tapers that fit within the diameters of the openings on the ends of the blank. As the illustration on page 106 shows, you fit the mandrels into the holes in the blank, then snug up the tailstock on the mandrel centers. That brings the holes in the blank into perfect alignment with the axes of the lathe. The outside of the blank can now be turned perfectly concentric with the bore so the walls are a uniform thickness.

Larger versions of a tapered mandrel can be used to hold large coopered items—that is, large cylinders made from narrow staves glued together the way barrels are made.

With coopered items, the mandrel is usually faceplate turned. It's more of a shouldered cap, with a good amount of taper on the tenon. I used this scheme many years ago to turn some 12" (305mm) diameter by 8' (2,438mm)-long coopered columns. I mounted the cap for the tailstock end on a faceplate, and then turned it to the size and shape I needed. For the other end, I bored a hole in the cap for the live center. I left the headstock cap on the faceplate and screwed both caps to the rough column before mounting it.

A tapered mandrel is also good for turning something like a napkin ring. Turn a spindle between centers, giving it a slight taper. The center of the spindle should match the inside diameter of the napkin ring. Slip the ring over the mandrel and remount it between centers. Tap the ring with a block of wood until it is well seated and runs true. Now turn the outside of the ring.

Tapered Mandrels

Tapered mandrels are jam chucks turned inside out. Just like a jam chuck, a 3° taper makes the work lock solid. Mandrels are good for holding napkin rings, pens, and porch columns.

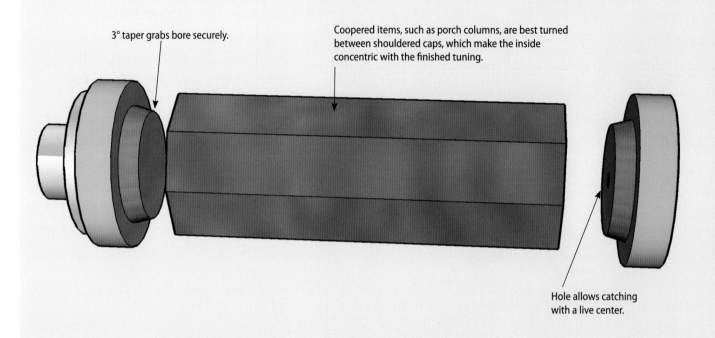

3° taper grabs bore securely.

Coopered items, such as porch columns, are best turned between shouldered caps, which make the inside concentric with the finished tuning.

Hole allows catching with a live center.

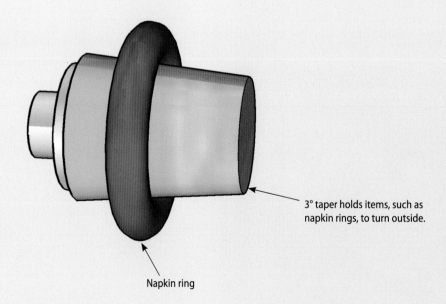

3° taper holds items, such as napkin rings, to turn outside.

Napkin ring

Coopered Birdhouse inspired by Andy Barnum

The diameter of the entrance hole and its height above the floor is critical for the type of bird you wish to attract. For instance, bluebirds like a 1¼" diameter hole that is 7" above the floor while a chickadee likes a 1⅛" diameter hole 6" to 8" above the floor. Google "hole diameters for birds" to find the details for just about any bird.

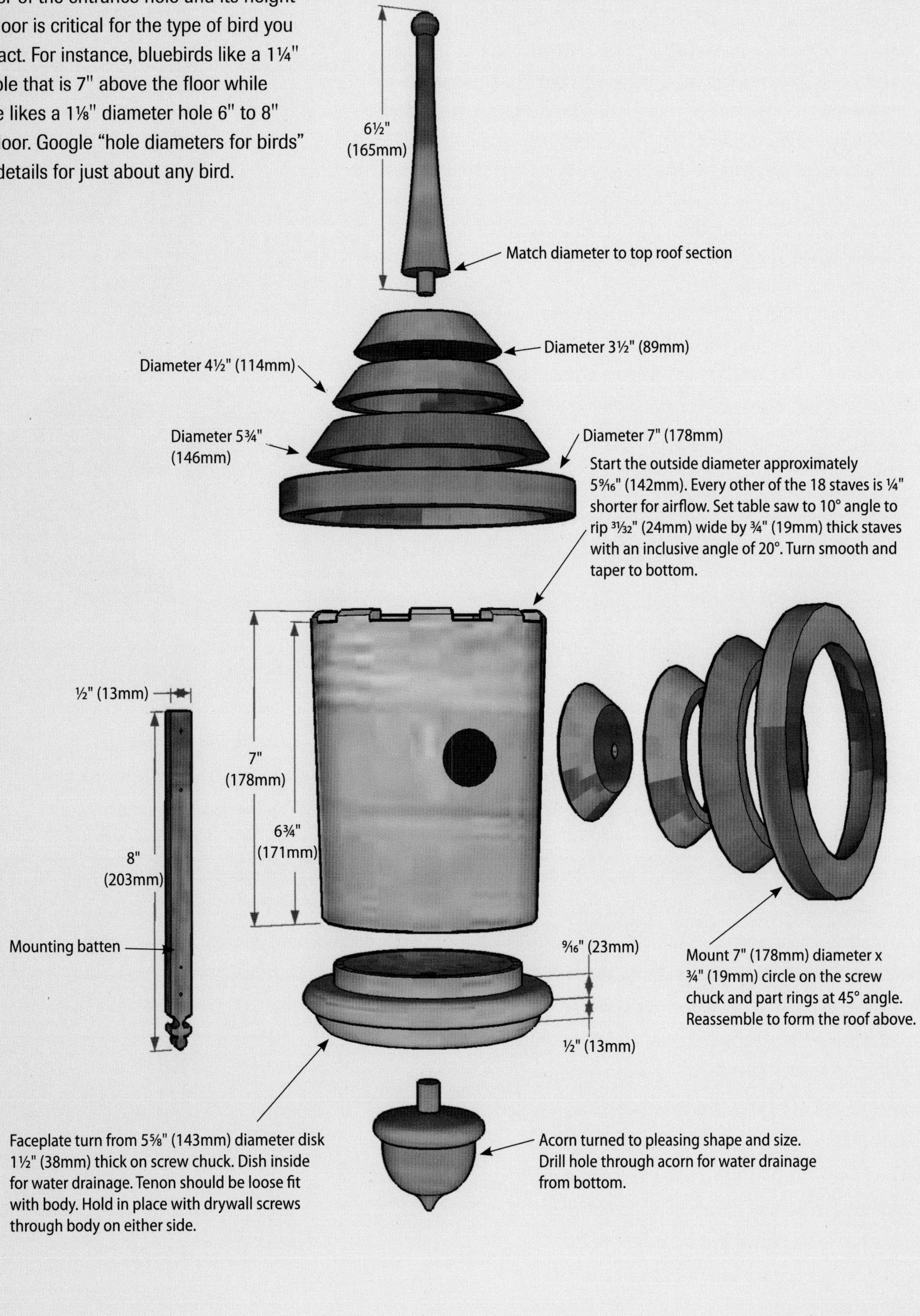

6½" (165mm)

Match diameter to top roof section

Diameter 3½" (89mm)

Diameter 4½" (114mm)

Diameter 5¾" (146mm)

Diameter 7" (178mm)

Start the outside diameter approximately 5⁹⁄₁₆" (142mm). Every other of the 18 staves is ¼" shorter for airflow. Set table saw to 10° angle to rip ³¹⁄₃₂" (24mm) wide by ¾" (19mm) thick staves with an inclusive angle of 20°. Turn smooth and taper to bottom.

½" (13mm)

7" (178mm)

6¾" (171mm)

8" (203mm)

Mounting batten

⁹⁄₁₆" (23mm)

½" (13mm)

Mount 7" (178mm) diameter x ¾" (19mm) circle on the screw chuck and part rings at 45° angle. Reassemble to form the roof above.

Faceplate turn from 5⅝" (143mm) diameter disk 1½" (38mm) thick on screw chuck. Dish inside for water drainage. Tenon should be loose fit with body. Hold in place with drywall screws through body on either side.

Acorn turned to pleasing shape and size. Drill hole through acorn for water drainage from bottom.

Pressure Chucks

Pressure chucks are an inexpensive and effective hold for production turning of plates, platters, trophy bases, and the like. At right top, we have just turned the bottom of a platter and are reversing it to turn the top side. The chuck is easily made by attaching a disk of wood to a faceplate and scraping it dead flat. A hole slightly smaller than a finish nail is drilled in the center and a finish nail is pounded in. The nail is now cut off about ¹⁄₁₆" proud and filed to a stubby point with the lathe running. The point ensures precise centering to layout marks and prevents lateral movement. The mark it leaves can be sanded out. A small square of wood is interposed between the live center and the work to prevent marring.

The same scheme, but without the nail point, works for natural edge bowls. Bowls are deep enough and the hold so brief that the nail is not needed. The block on the faceplate should be turned as close as possible to the shape of the inside bottom of the bowl. (Often a jam chuck can be used as the chuck.) Putting a piece of towel, leather, or even fine sandpaper between the chuck and the bowl makes for more positive drive and less marring of the work. Again a scrap of wood is interposed between the work and the live center. A pressure chuck allows dishing the base right up to the wood scrap. The area can be sanded out later.

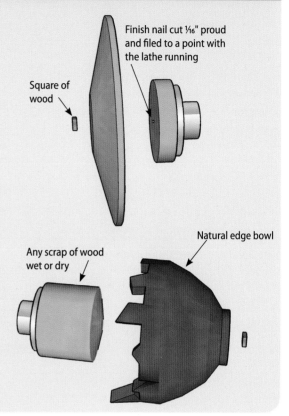

Finish nail cut ¹⁄₁₆" proud and filed to a point with the lathe running

Square of wood

Natural edge bowl

Any scrap of wood wet or dry

PRESSURE CHUCK

This is a close cousin of the jam chuck and can take myriad forms. A pressure chuck relies on pressure from the tailstock to hold the work against a *nest* mounted on the headstock spindle. In this case, a nest is a fixture that immobilizes the work, much the way a bird's nest keeps the bird from falling out of the tree. In turning, a nest can be a wood disk on a faceplate with either a finish nail protruding slightly at the center or strips of wood glued to the disk to surround the work.

To make another type of pressure chuck, turn a small dome, called a nubbin, that roughly mimics the inside form of a bowl. You now put some padding on the nubbin (a piece of old towel works well) and draw the tailstock up to pin the bowl on the nubbin. Put a small square of wood between the tailstock's live center and the center of the bowl base to leave the smallest mark possible. You can now finish the base of the bowl.

LOCKING NEST

This is a variation on a pressure chuck. It consists of a tapered wedge to lock the work in the nest. A locking nest is a great way to hold a square blank in place, without marring it with screw holes, while you turn a circular shape in it. With a locking nest, you can turn corner blocks for door or window trim, or make drink coasters with a depressed circular center that fits a glass or cup.

Locking Nest

A locking nest is great for turning corner blocks, coasters, and such. This one is to scrape a depression in a coaster to fit the glass. Gluing cork in the depression is a nice touch. Pieces can be loaded and unloaded quickly by tapping the wedge in and out. Speed should always be kept sensible with this chuck and no one should stand at right angles to it while it is turning.

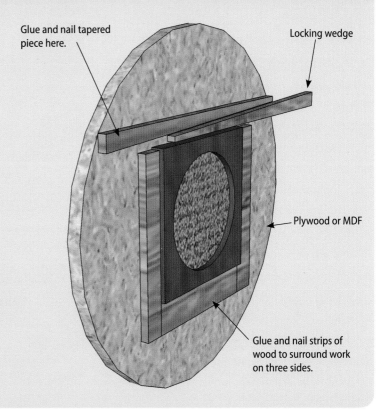

Glue and nail tapered piece here.

Locking wedge

Plywood or MDF

Glue and nail strips of wood to surround work on three sides.

Back View

Drill Pad Crotch Center

Begin by turning a spindle shaped like a #2 Morse taper, which will hold the drill pad. Once you get your wooden Morse taper close, make a line the length of it with a piece of white chalk. Now insert it in a #2 Morse taper socket and turn it a quarter turn. You will be able to see how good the fit is and where. Now you can put it back between centers and refine the taper. Keep checking with chalk until the chalk smears along the length of the turning.

Start with a 1" thick by 3" wide by about 12" long piece of wood and cut a 45° V down the middle. This is much safer than trying to put a V in a 3" square piece. Cut a 3" long section from the 12" and drill a ½" diameter hole in the center for a wood Morse taper.

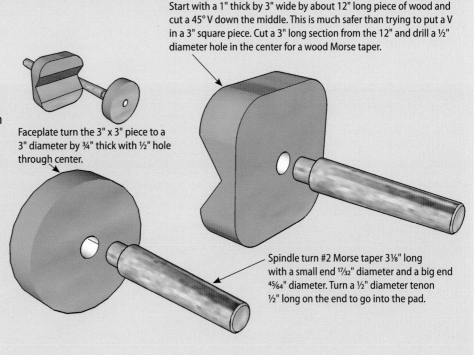

Faceplate turn the 3" x 3" piece to a 3" diameter by ¾" thick with ½" hole through center.

Spindle turn #2 Morse taper 3⅛" long with a small end $^{17}/_{32}$" diameter and a big end $^{45}/_{64}$" diameter. Turn a ½" diameter tenon ½" long on the end to go into the pad.

CHAPTER

DRILL PAD AND CROTCH CENTER

The drill pad and crotch center can turn your lathe into a horizontal drill press. Both chucks were standard accessories shown in old Delta tool catalogues.

Think of the drill pad as a small drill press table. Its Morse taper shaft fits into the tailstock. You mount a drill chuck with the bit you want to use in the headstock. Bring the tailstock up to the drill bit, holding the piece you want to drill against the pad. Turn on the lathe and advance the work into the drill by turning the tailstock handwheel.

Use the crotch center when you want to cross drill any round object on perfect center—drilling turned legs for a chair to accept tenons for the stretchers, for example. Use the crotch center with a drill chuck, just like the drill pad, keeping the round workpiece in the notch.

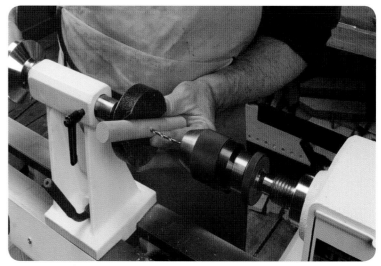

Using a crotch center. The notch in a crotch center supports round stock being drilled across its length.

Using a drill pad. Mounted in the tailstock, the pad supports the work to be drilled and keeps it on-axis. Advancing the tailstock moves the work into the drill.

Support for large turnings. Bedposts and other large turnings need extra support when being drilled. This V-block, attached to a post that fits in the banjo, does the trick.

Soft Jaws

Four-jaw scroll chucks generally come with one set of jaws that hold perfectly at about 1¾" diameter and a bit larger and smaller. The grip range of standard jaws is generally between about 1⅝" and 2¼" diameter. Jaws that hold down to about ⅜" diameter can be purchased separately.

It is often convenient to turn repetitive parts from a dowel. Some turnings, such as spindle-turned drawer pulls, incorporate a tenon of a specific diameter for later attachment to the drawer. An easy way to hold such items, without buying new jaws, is to turn a set of soft jaws.

In the the example at the right, I have turned a durable piece of wood to 1¾" diameter, mounted it in the scroll chuck and drilled a ⅜" diameter hole through it. I then used a back saw to cut kerfs to effectively turn it into a collet. I can now put a piece of dowel through it and it will hold fast when the chuck is clamped down on the soft jaws. They will leave no mark.

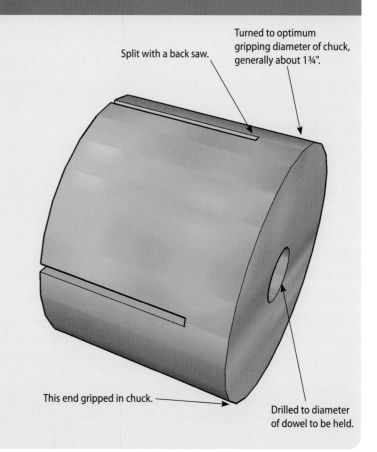

Split with a back saw.

Turned to optimum gripping diameter of chuck, generally about 1¾".

This end gripped in chuck.

Drilled to diameter of dowel to be held.

COLLET JAWS FOR A SCROLL CHUCK

A nifty trick for holding dowels is to make a set of collet jaws, also called soft jaws, for your scroll chuck. This can often help you avoid buying another set of jaws. The concept is simple and outlined in the illustration above. You can also use collet jaws to grab anything you do not want to mar, because it effectively turns your scroll chuck into a jam chuck.

The chuck is great for any serial production situation where you are turning parts that have a dowel of a specific diameter at one end. Examples are wine stoppers, which have a dowel that the cork fits over, or spindle-turned knobs, which have a dowel to facilitate mounting on the drawer. An advantage is that the chuck can be turned to the physical diameter of something like a knob base.

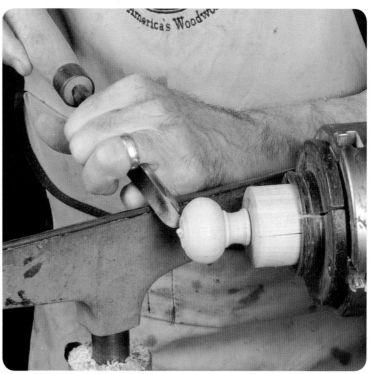

Using soft jaws. Shopmade soft jaws let you quickly turn multiple identical parts such as drawer knobs.

GLUE BLOCK

This is one of the most useful chucks for faceplate turning. The concept is simple—mount a disk of durable wood on a faceplate, scrape it flat, and glue the work to it.

The strength of the glue block comes from having the block's face grain glued to the face grain of the workpiece. If you are using seasoned wood, any glue will work as long as you give it enough time to cure: 24 hours, in most cases. With green woods, the handiest adhesive is cyanoacrylate glue. Purchase cyanoacrylate at hobby shops, woodworking supply stores, department stores, and by mail. It is available in a variety of viscosities; medium is best for wood.

Cyanoacrylate can be used in temperatures from 60° to 90°. It will dry in 5 to 15 minutes, depending on the temperature. It will not dry well at cold temperatures and should not be used below 60°F. As ambient temperature rises, setting times drop significantly. At 90°F it sets almost too swiftly. You can shorten setting times dramatically by spraying on an accelerator.

For a glue block that holds the work securely but also comes off easily and leaves the work undamaged, add kraft paper to the joint. A piece from a grocery bag works well. This is a great way to turn something like a tray, which needs a flat bottom.

Make sure the base of the tray is planed or sanded flat. Attach a glue block to a faceplate and scrape it flat. Now apply yellow or white carpenter's glue to the block and the workpiece and interpose the paper between the two during glue up. When you have finished the turning,

Bowl on a Glue Block

An excellent way to reverse chuck a bowl is with a glue block. The blank is mounted on a faceplate and the outside is turned. The foot or base of the bowl is scraped dead flat and a recess about 1½" to 2" in diameter is scraped about ⅛" deep. A disk of wood is mounted on a faceplate, scraped flat, and a shoulder is scraped so that the center area just fits the recess. There can be up to about ½₂" of play. The center should only be about ¹⁄₁₆" higher than the shoulder.

The center ridge is used to center the bowl and, in fact, cannot bottom out in the recess. The important detail is for the shoulder of the glue block and the bottom of the foot to be dead flat. Apply cyanoacrylate glue to the shoulder area and spray catalyst on the bowl. The two are pressed together quickly and firmly. Wait about 5 to 10 minutes and you can turn the inside of the bowl. Cyanoacrylate is the best choice because it works with green wood, which few other glues will do.

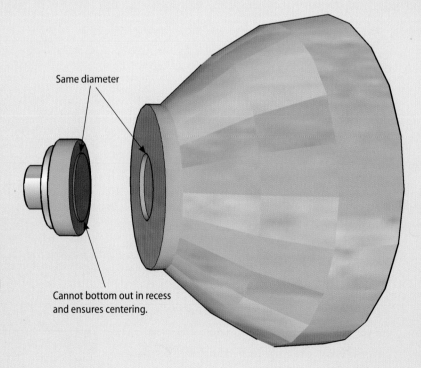

Same diameter

Cannot bottom out in recess and ensures centering.

Re-turning a Bowl Allowed to Air Dry Oval.

A good way to turn an air-dried bowl that is now oval a second time is to mount it on a glue block.

A good way to start the process is to pin the rough turned bowl against a nubbin as shown on page 108. Use a hook scraper (like the one I am grinding on page 52) to true the chucking recess from the rough turning process, which is now oval from drying more across the grain than along it. A light touch with the hook makes it round again.

Now use a chuck-making scraper to true and flatten the area around the recess for a perfect glue up.

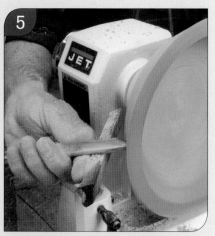

Make the glue block. Mount a scrap of hardwood that is larger than the bowl recess onto a faceplate. Scrape a tenon on the block that fits inside the recess in the bowl foot. Chamfer the tenon and see if the bowl will fit over it. Aim for a close fit. It can be as much as ⅜₂" (1mm) undersize. The tenon needs to be shorter than the depth of the recess in the bowl, with a square shoulder. Aim for ⅙" (2mm).

Glue the block onto the bowl. Apply glue only to the shoulder around the tenon and glue it to the bowl. I apply medium-viscosity cyanoacrylate glue to the glue block and spray catalyst to the bowl foot. Bring the two together with firm pressure and use the tailstock to maintain the pressure. That makes for a solid glue joint.

You are now ready to turn the outside and inside true and to a thin wall in the area of ½" (13mm) thickness. You will now have an air dried bowl that stays round for its life.

Split Turnings

Split turnings are a common furniture and architectural embellishment. The easiest and safest way to do them is to glue up the turning billet with brown kraft paper in the seam. Turning is then carried out normally. The finished turning splits easily off of the lathe by putting a chisel in the seam and tapping gently with a mallet.

This scheme also works for holding dry wood platters to a flat glue block for turning the top side. Once split from the glue block, the paper and glue can be sanded away with an orbital sander.

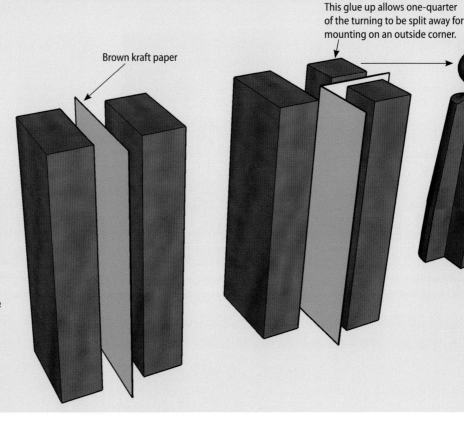

Brown kraft paper

This glue up allows one-quarter of the turning to be split away for mounting on an outside corner.

use a sharp wood chisel to pry off the glue block, and sand away the stray bits of paper and glue left behind on the work. A paper joint only works with dry wood, not green.

I lay out the circle for my tray with trammels or dividers on the side opposite the one planed flat and cut the circle on the band saw. During glue up, I find the center where my trammels indented the center of the circle and position this under my tailstock live center. I now use the tailstock to press the workpiece against the glue block, using the lathe like a bar clamp to center the work perfectly. I try to do this before leaving the shop for the day so that the setup is ready to go the next morning.

You can also use a paper joint in spindle turning. See the sidebar above.

STEADY REST

This is the only chuck that does not fit into the headstock or tailstock. Instead, it attaches to the lathe bed and supports a spindle in the middle, to prevent thin work from chattering against the turning tools.

A simple steady rest that is good for a one-time project turning a long piece is easy to make. See facing page for plans. It consists of a vertical bracket with a pivoting arm attached to it. The arm has a V-shaped notch cut in it at spindle height. Wedges hold the pivoting arm against the work. The trouble is, friction at the notch can quickly burnish or burn the work unless you apply liberal amounts of wax and keep the lathe speed slow.

Oneway sells a steady rest using wheels from inline skates to hold the turning. It works to perfection. If you expect to use a steady rest often, then consider buying the Oneway (or, if you feel inventive, think about devising your own).

Making Your Own Steady Rest

This steady rest appeared in Frank Pain's 1957 book, *The Practical Woodturner.* In use, the wedge is pushed down in back of the toggling V-block until the work is slightly deflected, thereby steadying it. This design is quite good for occasional spindle turning and can be improved by affixing ultra-high molecular weight (UHMW) plastic to the faces of the V.

I used this design to good effect when I turned 65 stair balusters. However, the rest will not tolerate speeds greater than about 800 rpm, and then only with liberal waxing of the V with paraffin. At higher speeds, it will burn the work.

The steady rest shown in the plan is tailored for a lathe with an 8" (203mm) center height and 1⅞" (48mm) spacing between the ways. You'll need to adjust the dimensions for your own lathe. The sides, back, and bottom parts of the rest are held together with finish nails and liberal amounts of yellow glue.

The V-notch needs to be at the lathe's exact center height. The eaiest way to position the V is to place the assembled rest on the lathe and swing the toggle past a point center to strike an arc on the wood. Place a compass on the arc and draw half a circle the same diameter as the work you plan to turn. Lay out a V that's tangent above and below the circle.

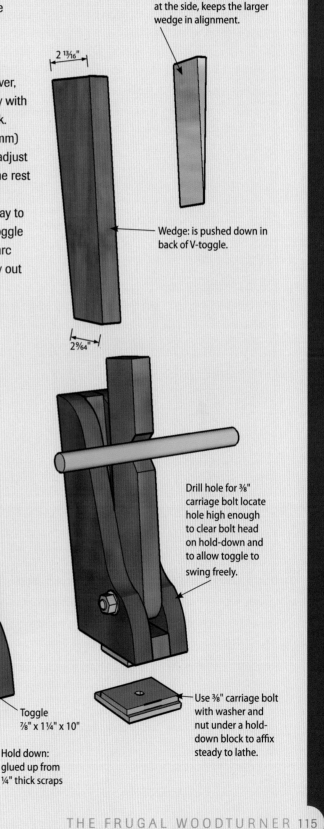

2 ¹³⁄₁₆"

Second wedge, pushed in at the side, keeps the larger wedge in alignment.

Wedge: is pushed down in back of V-toggle.

2 ⁹⁄₆₄"

⅞"

⅞"

⅞"

9⅝"

Drill hole for ⅜" carriage bolt locate hole high enough to clear bolt head on hold-down and to allow toggle to swing freely.

4⅛"

1⅞"

Toggle
⅞" x 1¼" x 10"

Hold down:
glued up from
¼" thick scraps

Use ⅜" carriage bolt with washer and nut under a hold-down block to affix steady to lathe.

2½"

2⅝"

Vacuum Chuck

A vacuum chuck can easily be shopbuilt. It is best tiled up from mitered pieces of a close grained, non-porous wood such as maple. I use eight tiles per layer of approximately 1"-thick wood. For eight tiles, each end is mitered to 22½°. I use three courses of tiles on a disk of ¾" medium density fiberboard, giving the chuck a total height of 3¾". Each course of tiles needs to be staggered from the one below because the end grain has no glue strength. Use a yellow glue such as Elmer's or Titebond. Once it is glued up, the chuck is scraped and sanded smooth on the inside and outside. Tiled work scrapes easily with a dome scraper. A cove for the sealing gasket is scraped in the nose of the chuck with a scraper ground specially for the job from any suitable blank of metal. The gasket is O-ring material and held in place with contact cement such as Pliobond. The resilience of O-ring material is measured on the Shore Durometer A Scale. The gasket must be about 30 durometers, while normal O-ring material is about 80. Packard Woodworks *(www.packardwoodwork.com)* sells suitable gasket material.

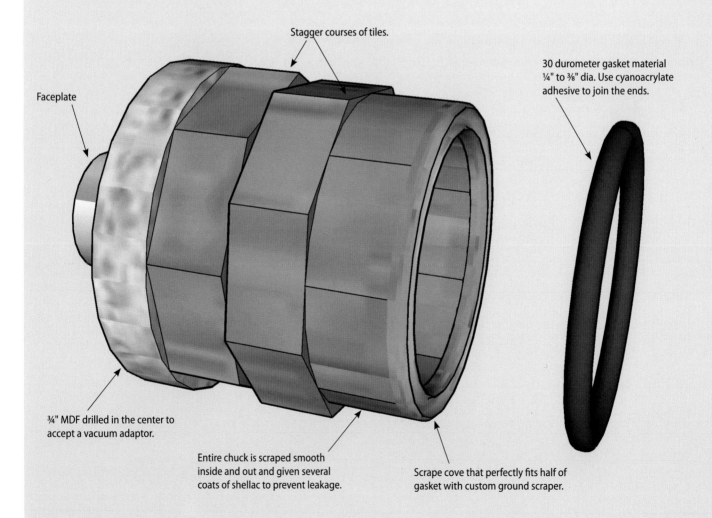

Stagger courses of tiles.

30 durometer gasket material ¼" to ⅜" dia. Use cyanoacrylate adhesive to join the ends.

Faceplate

¾" MDF drilled in the center to accept a vacuum adaptor.

Entire chuck is scraped smooth inside and out and given several coats of shellac to prevent leakage.

Scrape cove that perfectly fits half of gasket with custom ground scraper.

This design will grip the inside or outside of a bowl.

Vacuum Chuck Holding Powers

The table gives the approximate holding powers of chucks at sea level at vacuum settings. At standard conditions, air pressure at sea level is 14.7 pounds per square inch (psi) (1 kPa). For every 1,000 feet you work above sea level you reduce the holding forces of your vacuum chuck by 3.2%. For example, someone working in Denver would only achieve about 84% of the holding force listed because the 5,280-foot altitude brings air pressure down to 12.2 psi (0.8 kg/cm).

Diameter/Area of Chuck	Atmospheric Force: 28" HG (71 torr)/14.7 psi (101.4 kPa)	Atmospheric Force: 20" HG (508 torr)/9.8 psi (67.6 kPa)	Atmospheric Force: 16" HG (406 torr)/7.8 psi / (53.8 kPa)
3" dia. = 7 sq. in. (7.6cm/ 45.6 sq.cm)	103 lb = 47 kg	69 lb = 31 kg	55 lb = 25 kg
6" dia. = 28.3 sq. in. (15.3 cm/182.4 sq. cm)	416 lb = 189 kg	277 lb = 126 kg	221 lb = 100 kg

Rotary vacuum pump. This is the best type of vacuum generator for chucking.

VACUUM CHUCK

If your principal interest is turning bowls, a vacuum chuck is undoubtedly one of the most useful accoutrements. In my bowl-turning classes, the vacuum chuck quickly becomes the *suck chuck* and is in such demand, we dedicate a lathe to it full time.

Commercial vacuum chucks can cost as much as $950. However, if you make one, you can have this great chuck for $100 to $200. You need to acquire three major components.

The first and most expensive is the vacuum source. A rotary vacuum pump like the Gast Vacuum Pump is the best vacuum source. A Gast runs about $445, but you can buy essentially the same pump used from the Surplus Centers, in Lincoln, Neb., for about $55. You do have to wire the pump and it runs on 220 volts, neither of which is a deal breaker. The pump has other uses in a woodworking shop. My interest in vacuum veneering, for example, was mainly driven by the availability of my vacuum pump.

Next-best is a Venturi vacuum source, which connects to an air compressor and costs $40 to $125. A Venturi produces a high vacuum but does not pump much volume, which can be

problematic for lathe chucking. All woods have
some degree of porosity, especially through
end grain. Some vacuum loss due to bleeding
through the wood is inevitable, so you need a
good deal of suction volume to have consistent
and safe chucking. Venturi devices need about
80 psi (552 kPa) of air pressure at 2 to 6 cubic
feet per minute (0.057 to 0.17 cubic meters
per minute) to work. This makes a Venturi an
expensive way to make vacuum. The compressor
has to run a lot to generate the necessary vacuum.
Small compressors for nail guns do not produce
sufficient air volume to power a vacuum chuck.

The second chuck component is a vacuum
adaptor, a rotary connection that attaches to
the outboard end of the headstock spindle.
The adaptor allows vacuum to travel through
the spindle to the chuck itself. Oneway
manufacturing offers high-quality adaptors for
about $115. There are less-expensive alternatives.
One is the E-Z Vacuum Adaptor, which costs
about $85. It uses a piece of standard lamp rod,
which takes the vacuum from the rotary adaptor
to a fitting that nests in the Morse taper socket of
the spindle. Another is the Vacuum Adaptor Kit B,
from Packard Woodworks, about $60. It includes
some gasket material for sealing the chuck.

Think of the final necessity—the chuck itself—
as a cup, the base of which screws on the spindle
nose. The rim of the cup has a gasket to form
a seal between the chuck and the bowl you are
turning. The cup design allows a bowl to be
chucked with the base toward or away from the
spindle with equal ease. This makes it easier to
turn natural-edge bowls, which otherwise have to
be held in place with a pressure chuck.

The cup is the easiest part of a vacuum chuck
to make. All you need is a faceplate, some
gasket material, and wood for the cup itself. The
illustration on page 116 shows what to do.

Besides the main components, you will need
some vacuum line, a gate valve, some fittings, and

Using a vacuum chuck. Mount the chuck on the headstock and
connect the adaptor and hoses to the vacuum source. Then, as you steady
the work against the chuck, close the gate valve to turn on the vacuum.

a vacuum gauge. Standard air-compressor hose will work, but heavy polyvinyl chloride (PVC) hose costs less. Use standard compressed-air quick-connect fittings and buy a simple gate valve at any hardware store. Get a vacuum gauge from an industrial supply house for $15 to $20.

To chuck a bowl, place it against the chuck. If you have a known center point on the bowl, bring the tailstock up close, and center this spot under the point of the live center. Now turn on the vacuum, but to a low level so the chuck is just holding the bowl. I use about 5" Hg (127 torr) at this point. Turn the lathe spindle by hand, looking for any runout, or lack of centering. Tap the rim to correct runout, just as you would with a jam chuck. Once the bowl runs true, increase the vacuum to its maximum. If you are not pulling at least 16" Hg (381 torr), look for leaks.

If porous wood causes the leakage, rub on some oil finish. If that fails to produce a seal, you may need to switch to a different-sized chuck to correct how the bowl contacts the seal. If the leak comes from a small wormhole, bark inclusion, or dead knot in the bowl, there are several remedies. Press a packing peanut (the type that dissolves in water) into the hole. It can be washed out later. Or put thin plastic sheeting or kitchen plastic wrap over the defect. The vacuum will pull the patch into place. Or apply a thick coat of paste wax, which can be washed away with mineral spirits.

If you regularly use a vacuum chuck, you will soon remember to place a pencil against the center of the spinning work to make a distinct center mark before removing the work and re-chucking it. The mark makes it easy to replace the work in the chuck, and you can sand easily sand it away by hand later.

Necessary parts for a vacuum system. A vacuum adaptor (top) with a bearing around the air compressor fitting to allow it to turn independent of the lathe spindle. The fitting on the right end goes in a #2 MT and is connected to the bearing by lamp rod, which can be cut the length of your spindle. Also needed is a four way fitting called a cross, into which you connect the vacuum pump, the line to the adaptor, a vacuum gauge, and a ball valve. Opening the ball valve opens the system, causing the vacuum to drop to ambient pressure. Closing it partially causes partial vacuum and fully creates a full vacuum.

6 Simple, Inexpensive Finishes

After all of the work of turning and sanding, the high point of the process is applying the finish to the bowl or spindle you have just made. Catalogues and the woodworking press are resplendent with finishes and finishing techniques that all claim easy application and bulletproof results. I would like to share a couple of simple, easy-to-apply finishes that produce good results.

Shellac is a great, environmentally safe finish that can be applied with the work still on the lathe.

Build a Durable Finish with Shellac

A great spindle finish is a quick French polish using pure shellac thinned with some alcohol. With shellac, you only need to sand the work to about 180 grit. Sanding with finer grits is a waste of effort.

To use shellac, simply wipe or brush it on a completed turning and then turn on the lathe at a good speed. For a turning that is under 2" (51mm) in diameter, I run the lathe at 1,800 to 2,000 rpm. As the work spins, burnish the finish with wood shavings or a paper towel. The heat of the burnishing evaporates the alcohol and melts the shellac, bringing it to a superlative finish. If necessary, repeat the process once or twice to get the desired finish.

If you do not build a good finish easily, you have diluted the shellac too much. Add some of the concentrated solution and mix thoroughly. If the shellac smears in an unpleasing way, you have too thick a solution. Dilute it with more alcohol.

A classic French polish entails applying mineral oil to the wood, then the shellac. (You can buy mineral oil at any pharmacy.) In a few months' time, the oil brings out a beautiful patina in the wood. It is really worth the effort. The drawback to this old method is the mineral oil never dries and bleeds through the finish over time. You must clarify the finish several times after finishing by wiping it down with naphtha.

It's much easier to use an oil/varnish finish, which will dry under the shellac. Minwax Antique Oil Finish and Watco Danish Oil are both oil/varnish mixtures. Of the two, I prefer Minwax because it seems to build a suitable finish faster. The Minwax oil creates the same pleasing patina as mineral oil, but the finish does not need to be clarified. You can also make your own oil/varnish finish. See page 125.

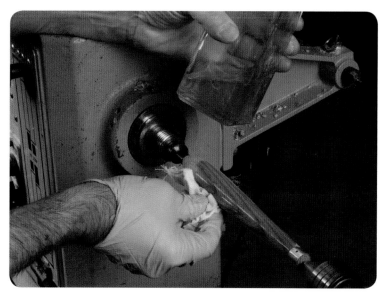

Wipe on. Once you have finished the turning, wipe on thinned shellac and start the lathe at a good speed. Use 1,800 rpm for a spindle less than 2" diameter.

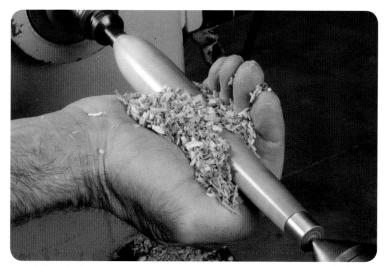

A quick polish. Use a handful of shavings to burnish the finished spindle and give it a subtle shine.

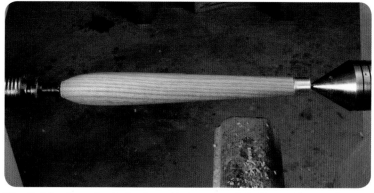

The finished product. Apply multiple coats of shellac until you achieve the desired depth of finish.

Mix Your Own Shellac

You can buy ready-to-use shellac at any hardware or paint store. However, the most economical way to get shellac is to mix your own: Buy flakes and dissolve them in denatured alcohol.

I buy pure shellac flakes from Homestead Finishing Products and make up a super-saturated solution by filling a pint or quart jar about two-thirds full of flakes and pouring in enough denatured alcohol to more than cover the flakes. I cap the jar and place it in a sunny window, shaking it every few hours. After 24 hours, I end up with about the equivalent of an 8-pound (3.6 kg) cut (8 pounds of flakes in a gallon of alcohol). I now pour the liquid into a new jar and dilute it 200%, adding twice as much alcohol as I did the first time, making a 2-pound (0.9 kg) cut.

Premixed shellac from the paint store has a one-year shelf life, but flakes last indefinitely. They also allow you to make as much or as little shellac as you need. The shellac you mix from flakes will last about six months.

Using flakes gives you more choices in the color of shellac, from blond (essentially clear) to garnet (a dark reddish tone). I use blond shellac on woods like walnut and cherry, and garnet on lighter woods such as maple. It does magical things to the grain and figure of curly maple.

Alcohol dissolves flakes. Fill a jar about one-third full of shellac flakes and then cover them with denatured alcohol. It takes about a day for the flakes to dissolve. The process goes a bit faster in a sunny window. Shellac, store-bought or home-brewed, only has a shelf life of six months to a year but lasts indefinitely in dry flake form. Therefore, making what you need as you need it is a great economy. You also get a much higher grade of shellac.

Polishing With Carnauba Wax

Another favorite finish of mine is pure carnauba wax, available at woodworking supply companies and finishing suppliers. A small piece will last for ages. Crayon it on a finished turning and burnish with shavings or a paper towel. Wax is a great finish in and of itself for small items such as pens and tree ornaments. It is also great over shellac, giving the work added gloss.

There are many expensive waxes on the market, all claiming to produce extraordinary results. The principal ingredient of all those products is carnauba wax. I think pure carnauba wax is superior. It produces a harder finish than other types of wax and is much cheaper.

With all wax finishes, sand the work well—to about 180 grit—for good results. The turning needs to be thoroughly burnished. Shavings work well, as does a paper towel. Never use cloth to burnish a turning. If it gets wrapped up in the work, it will drag your fingers with it.

Wax on. A stick of pure carnauba wax will last practically forever. Just rub some on the finished turning, then buff with shavings or a paper towel. You can use wax alone, or put it over a piece that has been finished with shellac.

Safe Oil Finishes

Oil is the preferred finish for most turners, especially those who make bowls. It causes a metamorphosis, making the beauty of the wood's grain and figure suddenly pop out at you. However, if the bowl is to be used for food service, you have to consider the toxicity of the finish.

The least toxic oils also leave the softest, least protective finish on the wood. Raw linseed oil and walnut oil, two popular finishes, are essentially nontoxic but soft and easily damaged. Linseed oil has been used as a laxative, and walnut oil is used in cooking.

The methods typically used to give oil more durability are boiling it or adding a catalyst, usually a heavy metal. Both alter the chemical structure of the oil, creating more sites on the oil molecules where they can cross-polymerize. Boiled linseed oil can still be purchased in any hardware store. While it was historically heated to achieve the desired effect, these days it is catalyzed. The heavy metal catalyst makes it unsafe to use around food.

For a durable finish that really brings out the character in the wood, most bowl turners use hardening oils such as Minwax Antique Oil Finish or Watco Danish Oil. They harden to a very durable finish, which will withstand sustained use and hand washing. Many woodturners believe the hardeners they contain remain locked inside the well-polymerized, durable finish. On most anything except a cutting board, the chemicals will not get into your food because they are encased in the finish.

When I apply an oil finish, I wear rubber gloves so I do not have to use lacquer thinner to remove dried finish. Wipe the oil on with a small rag and let it dry for 5 to 10 minutes, depending on the temperature—the hotter the weather, the quicker the drying time. When the oil is tacky, sand it with the same grit sandpaper you used at the end of

Making Your Own Oil/Varnish Finish

Increasingly strict environmental laws governing the amount of volatile organic compounds (VOC) that a finish can give off are making antique oil hard to find in some states. Sadly, I have not found a water-based product to produce the grain enhancement that oil does. A solution is to make your own. Here is my recipe.

1/3 Boiled Linseed Oil

1/3 Oil-based marine spar varnish

1/3 Mineral spirits

When you make a batch, either make it in small quantities or pour it into small containers that seal very well. This finish goes bad quickly once opened.

A word of caution when working with this finish. All oil finishes, including this one, have an affinity for oxygen and dry quickly; hence, they are susceptible to spontaneous combustion. Any rags, shavings, and paper towels used to apply the finish should be disposed of in a metal garbage can or outdoors. Do not leave them in the shop.

Add oil. Hardening oil provides a food-safe finish for turnings. Flood the piece with the oil, work it in with the same sandpaper you stopped sanding with, and apply more oil. Let it sit for a few minutes, then wipe away the excess. Repeat, using progressively finer grits of sandpaper, at 24-hour intervals.

dry sanding. Keep the sandpaper wet with mineral spirits. Apply another light coat of oil and wait until it gets tacky. Then use a paper towel to wipe off the excess.

Apply additional coats of finish, sanding each coat with progressively finer wet-dry sandpaper. When the oil gets tacky, wipe it with a clean paper towel. For a gallery-level finish, I machine sand the work to 180 grit, apply the first coat of oil, and then sand by handing using 220 grit. Doing so puts all of the sanding scratches in the same direction. I apply two to four more coats of oil, sanding with 320- and then 400-grit wet-dry paper. I allow 24 hours of drying time between coats.

All oil finishes have a tremendous affinity for oxygen and dry quickly. They are good candidates for spontaneous combustion. Any rags, shavings, and paper towels used to apply the finish should be disposed of properly. Let them dry outside, on the ground, or put them in a metal garbage can with a tight-fitting lid. Do not leave them in the shop.

Good Woodturning Setups for Three Budgets

The more money you can afford to spend on equipment, the easier it is to get started in woodturning, of course. But the less you have to spend, the more fun you can have—scouting out good used equipment (and feeling very smug when you have tracked down a real bargain), and taking satisfaction in the creation of your own chucks and scrapers.

When I wrote this book in 2009, it was possible to assemble a basic woodturning setup for as little as $500, and a good all-around setup for about $1,000. Inflation will hike those numbers as the years go by, I imagine. Even as prices change, though, the differences between the costs of basic, all-round, and upscale setups will likely remain constant.

Whatever your specific budget, I think it makes sense to devote about half to the lathe itself, spending the rest on tools and chucks.

The Conover Lathe. It was based on an idea popular in England through the 1930s. The one shown here was made about 1987. The Conover Lathe was a kit consisting of a high-quality headstock, tailstock, banjo, and tool rest that the user mounted on a wood bed that he made himself. The cast iron legs weighed 75 pounds each and added much bulk and stability. They were optional, however, and plans were supplied for the user to build a base with the bed timbers mounted on plywood pylons that were filled with sand. A benefit of the wood bed is that the length between centers was unlimited.

CHAPTER

Tight Budget/ Basic Setup

Lathe: Used full-size model or a new mini-lathe.

Tools: For bowl making, a ½" (13mm) bowl gouge and a 1" (25mm) or 1¼" (32mm) dome scraper. For spindle turning, ½" or ⁷⁄₁₆" (11mm) spindle or detail gouge, spindle roughing-out gouge, 1" (25mm) skew, parting tool.

Chucks and accessories: One or two inexpensive faceplates, plus a set of Beall spindle taps so you can make your own. An inexpensive pocket jig for sharpening.

Used lathes are reasonably easy to find and generally run one-half to one-fourth the original price. Assuming you have around $500 for a woodturning budget, that means spending about $250 on the lathe. You can buy a new mini-lathe for not much more, but as I explained in Chapter 1, a mini-lathe has limitations. If you can only afford one inexpensive lathe, buying a used full-size model makes a better investment.

The person selling the lathe is often as happy to see it get a good home as he or she is to receive a check. The seller may sometimes throw in some tools, chucks, a stand, and other accoutrements, increasing the value to you. A used lathe can be an exceptional value, but there are two provisos: Do not buy a lathe with a spindle size smaller than 1" x 8 tpi or a lathe that lacks Morse taper sockets in the headstock and tailstock.

Used gems: This older Nova 3000 is atypical of easy-to-find used lathes.

Options to look for. As with many other medium-priced new lathes designed in the last fifteen years, the Nova 3000 has a headstock that pivots to facilitate a greater swing for bowl work. The scheme works great to a point. You can turn large bowls and you will not have to remove the tailstock when you hollow them. However, small lathes are limited in the weight of the bowl blank they can handle.

Basic Tools for Bowls. For bowl turning, you simply need a ½" (13mm) high-speed steel bowl gouge and a large dome scraper (above). Improvise the other scrapers shown at right.

Good places to look for equipment are *craigslist.com* and your local chapter of the American Association of Woodturners. If you attend a woodturners' meeting and tell them what you are looking for, you will soon have a room full of enthusiasts beating the bushes for you. You can also find used lathes on eBay, but I do not think that is the best source. You cannot inspect the merchandise ahead of time and returns can be problematic. Unless the lathe is available locally, you will pay a lot of money for shipping. Finally, many of the sellers are retailers that use eBay as another store, so you will not get any break on the price.

The tools you need depend on whether you want to turn bowls, spindles, or both.

Bowl turning entails buying the fewest tools: one ½" (13mm) bowl gouge and one scraper, both in high-speed steel. In 2009 prices, those will cost $140 to $170. You can make any other scrapers you need.

A basic spindle-turning tool kit includes a spindle gouge or (my preference) a detail gouge, a spindle roughing-out gouge, a skew, and a parting tool. Buy them in high-speed steel. Expect to pay $115 to $250. Here, too, you can improvise any scrapers that you may need. Look for good used tools. It is possible to pick up decent skews and parting tools for a couple of bucks each.

Basic Tools for Spindle Turning. From bottom to top we have a ⁷⁄₁₆" detail gouge by Doug Thompson, an old Greenlee Diamond parting tool, a Sears HSS skew, and a Benjamin's Best 2" spindle roughing-out gouge. Again, improvise the scrapers.

Medium Budget/ All-around Setup

Lathe: Newer used lathe or a new mini-lathe.

Tools: Same as for tight and basic budget adding a beading and parting tool or an additional bowl gouge in ¼" (6mm) size.

Chucks and accessories: A couple of faceplates, plus a four-jaw scroll chuck. An inexpensive pocket jig and gooseneck jig for sharpening.

If you can afford to spend around $1,000, you have more choices. You can buy a new mini-lathe or a nice used lathe. I have seen used machines from manufacturers such as Nova, Delta, General, Jet, Sears, and Montgomery Ward. Again, be sure any used lathe you consider has a 1" x 8 tpi spindle. (Sears made many machines with ¾" x 16 tpi spindles that are not so usable.)

The tool selection is essentially the same as for the tight and basic budget. Put any money you save on tools into the lathe, which will pay dividends down the road as your skills improve. You can always add or upgrade tools as your budget allows. You may want to add a beading and parting tool or another size of spindle gouge.

New lathes, new options. The Jet is typical of a new mini-lathe with a bed extension and a stand that really put it in the full-duty category. The Jet makes an excellent spindle lathe but is a bit light for serious bowl work.

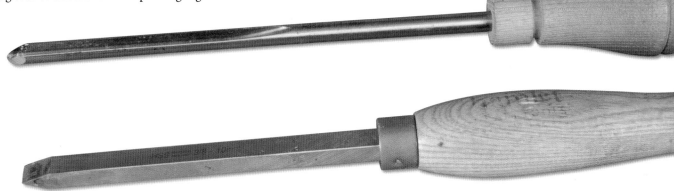

Basic kit additions. Although narrow gouges have a tendency to flex, especially if you take a heavy cut, a ¼" bowl gouge has sufficient stiffness to work well. By contrast, a ¼" spindle gouge is too small to work well at all.

Large Budget/ Upscale Setup

Lathe: New full-size model or a used top-line machine.

Tools: Same as for tight and medium budget.

Chucks and accessories: A couple of faceplates, a four-jaw scroll chuck, and a good set of sharpening jigs.

If you can afford to spend about $1,500 (in 2009 prices), you can put about $1,100 toward the lathe and still buy a good selection of tools and accessories. Consider new machines from Jet, Nova, and Delta. Alternatively, look for good deals on lathes that were top-of-the-line when new, from brands like Woodfast, Delta, Powermatic, and Vicmarc. Who knows? You may even run across a Classic Conover.

A larger budget doesn't necessarily mean buying more tools and chucks. The basic kit described will still suffice, although you may want to add a beading and parting tool or other sizes of bowl gouge. You can move up to bigger or better gear, buying a larger Nova, or Oneway scroll chuck, for example, instead of a small chuck. The same goes for your sharpening setup.

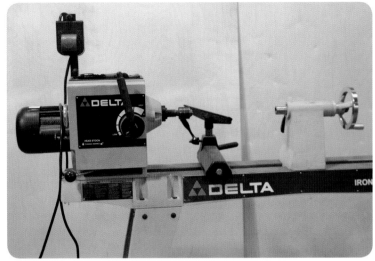

Used find. Although Delta has discontinued the 1440 full-size lathe, you can still find them new in the box on the used-tool market for a fraction of their original $1,200 price. The owner of the one shown here was asking only $500, for example.

Upscale additions. Useful additions to the basic kit on an upscale budget are a couple of faceplates (left) and a bigger chuck, such as the Oneway Stronghold (center), instead of a basic chuck, such as the Super Nova (far right). While making your own pocket jig and platform rest makes sense, a gooseneck jig like the Oneway at the bottom saves some time and effort.

The advantage of big. Nothing beats a big, heavy lathe for large faceplate work. Even in spindle work, mass is beneficial. Author Ernie Conover was on the design team for the Powermatic 3520b. Here, Patrick Brown tests the outboard capabilities of the unit during initial trials. It is often possible to find big heavy machines like this on the used market.

Appendix: Schools and Programs of Study

The following list covers a variety of training and educational programs. For a complete list of manufacturers and retailers mentioned in this book as well as other sources of supply, please log on to *www.foxchapelpublishing.com* and search product code "4345".

PROFESSIONAL ASSOCIATION

American Association of Woodturners
222 Landmark Center
75 West Fifth St.
St. Paul, MN 55102
www.woodturner.org
651-484-9094

INSTRUCTION

The following are woodworking schools that include woodturning among their courses. Also check offerings at local community colleges, local craft centers, or at organizations like the YMCA and YMHA; a number of them offer woodturning classes.

Anderson Ranch Arts Center
P.O. Box 5598
5263 Owl Creek Road
Snowmass, CO 81615-5598
970-923-3181
E-mail: Info@ andersonranch.org
www.andersonranch.org

Arrowmont School of Arts and Crafts
556 Parkway
Gatlinburg, TN 37738
www.arrowmont.org
865-436-5860

Center for Furniture Craftsmanship
25 Mill Street
Rockport, ME 04856
207-594-5611
E-mail: cfc@woodschool.org
www.woodschool.org

Connecticut Valley School of Woodworking
249 Spencer St.
Manchester, CT 06040
www.schoolofwoodworking.com
860-647-0303

Conover Workshops
P.O. Box 679
Parkman, OH 44080
www.conoverworkshops.com
440-548-3491

Craft Supplies USA
1287 E 1120 S
Provo, UT 84606
800-551-8876
E-mail:
workshops@woodturnerscatalog.com
www.woodturnerscatalog.com

The Ellsworth School of Woodturning
1378 Cobbler Rd.,
Quakertown, PA 18951
www.ellsworthstudios.com
215-536-5298

John C. Campbell Folk School
One Folk School Road
Brasstown, NC 28902
www.folkschool.org
800-365-5724

Kelly Mehler School of Woodworking
P.O. Box 786
Berea, KY 40403
www.kellymehler.com
859-986-5540

Marc Adams School of Woodworking
5504 E. 500 N.
Franklin, IN 46131
www.marcadams.com
317-535-4013

North Bennett Street School
39 N. Bennett Street
Boston, MA 02116
617-227-0155
E-mail: workshop@nbss.org
www.nbss.org

Penland School of Crafts
P.O. Box 37
67 Dora's Trail
Penland, NC 28765
828-765-2359
E-mail: info@penland.org
www.penland.org

Index

Acquisition editor: John Kelsey
Copy editor: Kerri Landis
Cover designer: Lindsay Hess
Designer: Dan Clarke
Editors: David Heim, Paul Hambke
Editorial assistant: Liz Norris
Proofreader: Lynda Jo Runkle
Indexer: Jay Kreider

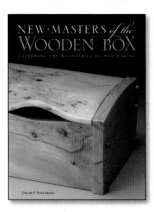
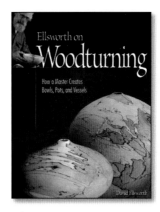

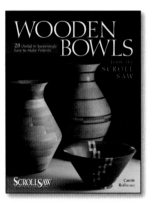
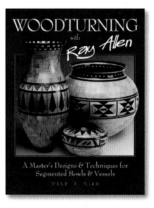